FOUR AMERICAN INVENTORS

FOUR AMERICAN INVENTORS

BY

FRANCES M. PERRY

YESTERDAY'S CLASSICS

CHAPEL HILL, NORTH CAROLINA

This edition, first published in 2011 by Yesterday's Classics, an imprint of Yesterday's Classics, LLC, is an unabridged republication of the text originally published by American Book Company in 1901. For the complete listing of the books that are published by Yesterday's Classics, please visit www.yesterdaysclassics.com. Yesterday's Classics is the publishing arm of the Baldwin Online Children's Literature Project which presents the complete text of hundreds of classic books for children at www.mainlesson.com.

ISBN: 978-1-59915-412-1

Yesterday's Classics, LLC
PO Box 3418
Chapel Hill, NC 27515

CONTENTS

ROBERT FULTON

ELI WHITNEY

SAMUEL F. B. MORSE

THOMAS A. EDISON

THE STORY OF
ROBERT FULTON

ROBERT FULTON

CHAPTER I

A BOY WITH IDEAS

The schoolmaster had left the high stool at his high desk and was walking down among the benches where the boys sat. Most of the pupils looked up to see what he would do.

There was one who did not look up. That boy's curly head was bent over an old book in which he was drawing something. He was so busy that he seemed to have forgotten where he was.

The master stopped beside his bench and looked over his spectacles severely at the boy, who started quickly and held up his work for the teacher to look at. His eyes were glowing with satisfaction, and said as plainly as lips could say, "Is it not good?"

The drawing was well done. It was so good that the master could not scold, but he thought it was his duty to teach the boy to do more useful things. He did not praise him, therefore, but said gravely, "It would be better for thee, Robert, to spend thy time studying thy books."

"I know it, sir, but my head is so full of my own

ideas that there seems to be no room in it for ideas from books," answered the boy.

This is one of the stories that the schoolmates of Robert Fulton used to tell about him after he had become famous. It happened long ago in a little Quaker school in Lancaster, Pennsylvania, where Robert Fulton spent his schooldays.

He was born on the fourteenth of November, 1765, on a farm in the township of Little Britain, in Lancaster County. Mr. and Mrs. Fulton were quiet, modest people, and little dreamed that the name of the township would one day be changed in honor of their baby, who kicked and crowed in his old-fashioned, hooded cradle just like any ordinary baby. But the name was changed and the township where the great inventor was born is now called "Fulton."

When Robert was less than a year old his father sold the farm and moved to Lancaster, the county seat. There Mr. Fulton died about two years later, and Mrs. Fulton was left with a small income to bring up her five young children. As Robert was the oldest boy he grew up with the understanding that he must do something to support the family.

His mother knew how to read and write, and she taught him at home with his sisters until he was eight years old. Then she sent him to school.

His teacher thought him a dull pupil, but found him quick enough at everything except his lessons.

One day the worthy man punished him by striking

his hands with a ruler. This was no uncommon occurrence, but it made Robert angry and he said with spirit, "Sir, I come here to have something beat into my head and not into my hand."

At another time when asked why he came late to school, he held up a lead pencil and answered, "I have been to the smith's pounding out lead for this pencil, and it is a good one too."

That was doing something useful, and it pleased the teacher. He praised Robert, and the boys begged him to make pencils for them.

Out of school he was looked upon as unusually bright and promising. He was witty and good natured, and every one liked him. He was fond of visiting shops and talking with the men. He was a great pet among them and they not only answered his questions, but sometimes let him use their tools. In that way he learned much more than most boys know about machinery and various trades.

CHAPTER II

WORKING OUT SOME OF THE IDEAS

As Robert Fulton grew older he did better work at school. His quickness in numbers often surprised his teacher, and his school papers were always neat and beautiful.

Still he found more to do out of school than in school. He spent much time drawing; and he improved in that art constantly, although he had no instruction in it.

When he was eleven years old a terrible war broke out between the American colonies and England. A few of the colonists were loyal to the king, but many wanted a new and independent government.

In Lancaster there were Tories, who took the king's part, Quakers, who thought war wicked, and patriots, who were ready to fight for liberty.

There was great excitement everywhere. British or colonial soldiers encamped in many of the towns. Men and boys went to war, leaving behind weeping wives, mothers, and sisters.

Robert Fulton's father was dead, and he and his brothers were not old enough to go to the war. But young as he was he loved his country and wished the colonists to win. He never missed an opportunity to show his patriotism.

Just before the Fourth of July, 1778, a notice was put up requesting the citizens of Lancaster not to illuminate their houses as usual in celebration of the day, since candles were very scarce.

Robert was sorely disappointed. The Fourth was a great day to him. He remembered the first Fourth-of-July just two years before. How the bells had rung! How the windows had gleamed with candles! How the streets had blazed with bonfires and how joyous the people had been!

This year he had his candles ready, and had been anxiously awaiting the day. He was not the kind of boy to act against the wishes of the city officers. That would have been a poor way to honor his government's birthday. Yet he did not want to give up his celebration altogether.

After thinking about it for a while he took the candles back to the shop and exchanged them for pasteboard and gunpowder. He took these to the barn and worked quietly the rest of the day.

On the evening of the Fourth he brought out some queer-looking pasteboard tubes with slender sticks in them. When a lighted candle was applied at one end— whizz! away went the stick with a great train of sparks against the black sky.

The home-made rockets were a surprise to the people of Lancaster. Robert thought them much better than candles.

It would not be safe for every thirteen-year-old boy to make his own fireworks, but Robert knew something about gunpowder. He understood just how much to use and where to put it. He had heard about sky rockets and had an idea how they were made. He drew a plan of one and, before attempting to make any, found out by arithmetic how large a charge of powder to use.

In the war times there were many gunsmiths in Lancaster whose shops were kept open day and night; for the government was in great need of arms for the soldiers.

Robert was so deeply interested in guns that he soon knew more about the making of them than many of the craftsmen who did the work. He made nice drawings of guns, showing all the parts and the use of each. In some of the drawings he showed how the pieces might be made stronger or more beautiful by the addition of certain new parts or ornaments.

When he showed these pictures or plans to the gunmakers they often made use of his suggestions, and found that they improved their arms by doing so.

But there were other ways in which Robert surprised the gunmakers. He could estimate with figures the distance that a musket of given measurements would send a ball. When the gun was finished and the men went out into the field to try its power, they usually found that young Fulton's figures were correct.

At this period of his boyhood he frequently went to a drug store to buy quicksilver. His friends were curious to know what he wanted it for, but no one could find out. They questioned and teased and joked in vain. At last they gave up trying to discover his secret. But they paid him for his silence by calling him "Quicksilver Bob." It was not a bad nickname for him, for his brain and his fingers were as active as quicksilver.

In his sixteenth summer Robert was invited by one of his boy friends to go on a fishing trip. His mother was willing to have him go, for the other boy's father would be with them. Moreover they were going up the Conestoga River to a point not far from the home of one of Robert's aunts, and he promised to make her a visit.

He started off in high spirits. For a while he enjoyed the view of the clear stream with its wonderful reflections of grassy hill slopes and overhanging trees. He forgot about gun shops and was content to sit by the hour holding a fishing rod. But at length he began to think of making something, and became restless.

When he and his friends went out on the river to fish they were obliged to use a clumsy square fishing boat. In order to move it from one place to another the boys had to pole it. That is, they stood on the boat and pushed against a long pole with which they could reach the bed of the stream. That was a slow way of getting along and it was a hard one, too.

One afternoon it occurred to "Quicksilver Bob" that the boat could be moved in a much easier way. He was anxious to try it, and started off at once to his aunt's to make the promised visit and some experiments.

While there his aunt saw but little of him. He spent his time tinkering in the attic, and before he left he had made a toy boat that could be moved about on the water with tiny paddle wheels. He showed it to his aunt and asked her to take good care of it till he came again. He then got together such materials as he wanted and bade good-by to his relative.

As soon as he rejoined his comrade he told him that he had a plan for moving the fishing boat without so much labor. When the boy learned what the plan was, he was as anxious as Robert to try it.

Both went to work making paddle wheels. They were very rough wheels, made by fastening together at the center two slender poles at right angles to each other. At the four ends of the two poles the boys nailed flat boards or paddles. They put one of those wheels on each side of the boat and fastened them to the ends of a long rod running through the boat. The rod was bent so that it could be turned by a double crank.

"She goes ahead all right," said Robert's friend, Christopher, as the young inventor tried the new craft for the first time. "But how shall we guide her?"

"Oh, I have thought of that," answered Robert. He took a contrivance, not unlike an oar-lock, out of his pocket and fastened it to the stern of the boat. By the help of a paddle working in this socket one could guide the boat while the other turned the crank. They found the paddle wheels a great improvement on the pole.

FULTON'S FIRST EXPERIMENT WITH PADDLE-WHEELS

"Why didn't *you* think of that, Christopher?" asked Christopher's father, looking on with admiration.

"I wonder why I didn't," answered the boy. "It looks easy enough now that Bob has shown me how."

Robert might have told them this story of Columbus and the egg: One day at the table some men were saying that it was no great thing to sail across the Atlantic Ocean; they could do it themselves. In reply to their remarks Columbus picked up a boiled egg and asked which of them could make it stand on end. All tried in vain. "And yet," said the great man, "it is easy enough, and you can all do it when I have shown you how." With that he set it down so hard as to crush the end a little. And the egg stood in its place straight and steady.

CHAPTER III

THE YOUNG ARTIST

Robert Fulton had been much with people older than himself. As a result he was unusually sensible and dignified, and appeared older than he really was. At the age of seventeen he thought himself quite a man, and set out to make his own living.

He determined to be an artist. He liked to draw and paint, and spent many hours with pencil and brush, making drawings of machinery or painting pictures. He was successful with both landscapes and portraits. Nothing was too difficult for him to attempt. A picture that he painted during the war represented the Whig boys of Lancaster as vanquishing the Tory boys in a fight. It was exhibited and attracted a good deal of attention.

Although he had had no instruction in the art of painting, he had some talent, and his friends in Lancaster thought his work very good. They called him a second Benjamin West.

Benjamin West was a gifted artist. He was brought up in a plain Quaker home not far from Lancaster. From boyhood he had wanted to be an artist but every one

BENJAMIN WEST

discouraged him. Notwithstanding the disapproval of his family and his friends he struggled on. He went to England. There he became famous. He received large sums of money for his pictures which were bought by the rich and noble.

His old neighbors heard of his success with surprise, and for a while every boy who could draw hoped that he too might become a famous artist.

Robert Fulton had been encouraged by the success of Mr. West to give much attention to art. He had confidence in his own talent, but when he saw a fine picture he realized that his own work was very crude. He resolved to go to Philadelphia to study.

He spent four years there, studying and painting. His work found many admirers. He soon gained a reputation as a miniature painter. He sold pictures almost as fast as he could paint them. In that way he was able to pay his own expenses and save money.

When he was twenty-one years old he went back to Lancaster to visit his mother. He had saved about four hundred dollars, and with that he bought her a farm in Washington County in the southwestern part of Pennsylvania. It was a good farm of about eighty acres. It had been cleared and the house and barn had been built. The purchase was a wise investment. With a little help Mrs. Fulton and her daughters could make a comfortable living on the farm.

Her son knew that it would be hard to move. The way was long and the roads were poor. Rivers and mountains had to be crossed. He therefore went with the family to see them comfortably settled in the new home.

The journey was made in early summer, and it was a pleasant one. Mrs. Fulton was happy to have her manly son with her again even for a short time. It was satisfying to feel that she was on her way to take possession of a farm of her own. All of them, but especially the young artist, enjoyed the picturesque scenery through which they passed.

The farm was just what Mrs. Fulton had often longed for. All worked with a will, and they soon had the house and the garden in good order. Neighbors came from distant farms to welcome them.

Robert felt sure that his mother and sisters would be happy and comfortable in their new home. He could go back to Philadelphia with a light heart. He felt that he ought to go without further delay.

Mrs. Fulton did not wish her brilliant son to stay on the farm and plow. She was proud of him and wanted him to go to the city and become great and famous. Yet it was hard to say good-by, for it would be a long time before she would see him again.

On his return journey Robert Fulton rode through large tracts of rich, wild land. "Much of this land would make fertile farms," thought he. "But of what use would it be to raise a crop here? How could the farmer get it to market?"

That question came back to him again and again, and some years later he tried to answer it.

Mr. Fulton had made many warm friends in Philadelphia. Those who understood his work best and valued it most highly advised him to go to England. He realized that he could make no further progress in Philadelphia, and decided to go abroad.

He wrote to the great Benjamin West, who promised to help him if he would go to England. As soon as his resolution became known, his friends in Philadelphia gave him letters of introduction to their friends in England and France. So he did not feel as if he were going altogether among strangers.

He crossed the ocean on a large ship with great white sails. When the sun was bright and a favorable breeze blew, the sails were filled with wind and the vessel flew like a bird over the blue waves. When a storm arose the sails had to be taken in, and the naked masts creaked and the wind whistled through the rigging. At other times there were days of calm when almost no breeze was stirring, and the great sails hung limp and motionless, and the ship floated idly on the sea.

After a long voyage the cry of "Land!" brought all the passengers on deck. Robert Fulton stood among them looking eagerly at the shores of the Old World. There he hoped to see wonderful pictures and meet renowned artists. He told himself that he would learn all they had to teach him, and that one day his work might be celebrated.

The ardor of the young artist was not soon dampened. Mr. West treated him with the greatest kindness. He invited him to his home and introduced him to his friends. He was pleased with his young countryman's pictures, and praised their beauty while he pointed out their faults.

The two artists became very fond of each other; they worked and walked and talked together in perfect good fellowship.

With such a powerful friend to introduce him, Mr. Fulton became acquainted with influential men who liked his work and bought his pictures. Every one that met the handsome young American liked him. Strangers were pleased with his fine face and his frank manly manner. When they knew him better they found he could talk as well as he could paint. And best of all, he proved to be a grateful, true, and generous friend. He was impulsive and warm hearted. He loved and trusted those whom he admired, and they could not help loving him in return.

CHAPTER IV

THE ARTIST BECOMES AN ENGINEER

Among Mr. Fulton's new friends there were many who, while somewhat interested in art, were much more interested in other subjects. They liked the young artist the better when they found that he knew about other things besides painting.

Mr. Fulton met, among others, a duke who had given a great deal of attention to canals. As he listened to the nobleman talk he said to himself, "I have found the answer to the question, 'How can the farmers on inland farms of Pennsylvania get their produce to market?' "

The duke was pleased to find Mr. Fulton such an eager listener. Later he was more delighted to hear his clever and original suggestions about canals. He thought that the clear and perfect drawings which he made to explain his ideas were more interesting than the finest paintings.

The two men formed a friendship that became stronger as years passed.

Mr. Fulton, having had his interest in canals aroused, could not drive the subject from his mind. Nor did he wish to do so. To supply the farmers with a cheap and quick means of carrying their produce began to seem a more important matter than painting beautiful pictures.

The principal cities and villages in America were built on the coast or on rivers. Even farmers chose land near navigable water. For supplies were carried from the country to the city and from the city to the country in sloops, schooners, and barges.

Most of the transportation between places away from the water was done by wagons. Men, called teamsters, made a business of hauling goods from one place to another. There were few good roads in America then, for it took a great deal of money to make them. For that reason it cost almost as much as produce was worth to have it hauled to market by horses and wagons.

Some artificial water-ways had been built between places where there were no natural ones. These were called canals. The large freight boats used on them were pulled or towed by horses driven along a path on the bank of the canal. Heavy loads could be transported in that way at small cost. But such canals as were then built were so large and expensive that it was impossible to have many of them.

Mr. Fulton thought the canal was the most practical means known for conveying produce from one part of the country to another. And he was probably right. If you were to take a journey along the Erie Canal to-day, you would find that there are many who still use canals in preference even to railroads. In the summer and fall many fleets of grain barges towed by steam tugs pass along this canal.

But Mr. Fulton knew that his countrymen could not afford to build large canals in all the places where canals were needed. He thought that it would be better to make them smaller and to have more of them.

He wrote a book to explain his idea of an extensive system of small canals joining farms and villages. In the book he showed that such a system would not only benefit those who used the canals but would strengthen the nation. It would increase the value of the public lands in the interior. It would bring the people of different sections of the country into closer relations. They would have common business interests, and the Union would therefore be strengthened.

He showed how canals could be more simply made, and suggested improvements in canal boats.

If a canal should open into a river its waters would join those of the river and flow away towards the sea. So when a canal comes to a stream its waters have to be confined in a great, strong trough that crosses the river just as a bridge does. This is called an aqueduct. Aqueducts were made of stone in Fulton's time and were very costly.

Mr. Fulton thought they could be made of cast iron instead of stone. Others said that iron could not stand the changes in temperature and would break. But one of the stone aqueducts was destroyed in a flood and the men who rebuilt it followed Mr. Fulton's plan. The iron aqueduct wore so well that others were made like it. Afterwards iron was used commonly for that purpose.

Another expensive feature in canal building is the arrangement by which boats are raised and lowered from one section of the canal to another. Canals have to be level. There can be no slope to them as there is to a river. If the land slopes up, the canal is built in a series of level sections, each higher than the one before it.

It is customary to build locks for moving boats from one level to another. They are large, square tanks rising gradually like steps.

When a boat from above comes to one of these giant stairways its way is barred by big gates. These gates open

LOCKS, AND BOATS GOING DOWN

inward and the pressure of the water against them holds them shut. Every one of the tanks or locks has a pair of these gates. They are all closed. When the boat is ready to go down, the valves of the canal gates leading to the first lock are opened. The water flows from the canal into this lock until it is as high in the lock as it is in the canal. The pressure of the water on both sides of the gates is then equal and the gates can be opened.

The boat passes into the lock and the gates behind it are closed. The valves in the gates leading to the next lower lock are opened and the water flows out of the first lock into the second until it is even in both. The gates are opened; the boat goes into the second lock and so on, until it is "down stairs."

If the boat is to go up it enters the lowest lock. The gates are closed back of it; the valves of the upper gates are opened and the water runs from the upper into the lower lock until the water in both is level. Then the gates are opened and the boat goes into the higher lock. Thus step by step it climbs the hill.

Mr. Fulton thought that where locks were needed in small canals they should be made of wood instead of stone. But he believed that only a few of them, were needed.

He planned a cheaper way of moving canal boats from one level to another. His plan was to use double tracks on a sloping surface. One end of the tracks would be in the lower section of the canal; the other in a lock leading to the upper branch.

FULTON'S DOUBLE-INCLINED PLANE

When a boat wanted to reach the upper section of the canal a stout car or truck was sent down the slope into the water and the boat was floated upon it. This car was connected by a long chain that passed over a pulley at the top of the hill, with another car on the parallel track. The chain was so long that when one car was at the bottom of the slope the other was at the top. A heavy weight was kept on the second car, and when the car with the boat on it was ready to be brought up hill the weight on the other car was increased until it was greater than the weight of the boat. Then it began to go down hill, and as it went down it drew the car with the boat on it up. When it was in the lock the lower gates were closed and the valves in the upper gates were opened. The lock was filled with water and the boat could be taken on its way in the higher section of the canal.

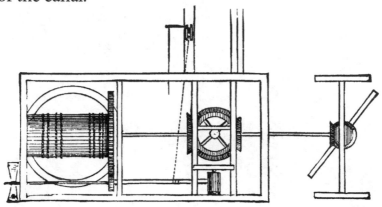

DETAILS OF FULTON'S INCLINED PLANE

Mr. Fulton's views attracted much attention, and his suggestions were tried in many places with success.

He gave more and more time to engineering and less and less to art. At length he decided that he would make engineering rather than painting his life work. His skill with the pencil was by no means lost in his new business. He found it a great help in illustrating and explaining his plans.

While in England he invented and received patents for several improvements in canals and canal boats. He also invented a mill for sawing marble, a machine for spinning flax, and a machine for removing earth from canal beds.

When he left that country he was well known as an earnest promoter of the useful arts.

CHAPTER V

EXPERIMENTS

In 1797 Mr. Fulton left England to go to France. For some years he lived in Paris in the same house with Joel Barlow, a prominent American statesman and poet of that time. The two men formed a warm friendship. Mr. Fulton illustrated Barlow's greatest poem, the "Columbiad," which was dedicated to him. They worked together and were partners in many business ventures.

Robert Fulton's head was still very full of his own ideas, but he now thought it worth while to try to find room in it for some ideas from books. He studied mathematics, science, and foreign languages.

To earn money to pay his expenses he painted a panorama. The people of Paris had never seen one before. They thought it was very entertaining to see a story told in a succession of beautiful pictures, and went in large crowds to see it.

Study and painting were merely his pastimes, however. He gave his serious attention to making experiments. He seemed to be no longer interested in finding a way for his countrymen to transport food and clothing and other necessities of life. He was trying to find a way to blow up warships.

You remember that in his boyhood days during the Revolution, he had spent hours in the gunsmiths' shops. Even then he had realized that gunpowder was a marvelous power, and he had discovered that man can measure and direct its force. He believed that new ways of controlling and using that force ought to be discovered.

He contrived a torpedo that would explode some minutes after the machinery attached to it had been set in motion. He then went to work to make a diving boat in which men could move about under water. With one of these boats a few men could go under a warship and fasten a torpedo to it. When they had it firmly fixed where they wanted it, they would start its machinery. They would have time to get well out of the way before the explosion.

He spent much money and time in his experiments with the diving boat and the torpedoes. He tried to interest the French and English governments in his inventions. Committees were appointed to see whether his invention was of any value. They found it to be all that Mr. Fulton claimed, but they did not like the idea that their splendid warships could be destroyed by a few men. It seemed to them that this invention would put too much power into the hands of the weak.

That had been Robert Fulton's idea in working with the torpedo and diving boat. In those days the seas were ruled by the nations that had the most warships. Many

FULTON'S SUBMARINE BOAT
(FROM AN OLD CUT)

wrongs were suffered at sea by the traders of smaller nations whose navies were not strong. Troubles were constantly arising because of wrongs done at sea.

Mr. Fulton thought that if it were possible for a few men to destroy a warship the owners of the great warships would cease doing injury to others. For their own safety the strong would be obliged to agree to fair and just laws governing ocean trade.

So after all, in spite of first appearances, Robert Fulton was still struggling with the old question of how to help along transportation by water.

He had faith in his invention and in its usefulness to men. On one occasion he was offered a reward if he would keep his invention out of use in all countries.

He answered this offer in a very emphatic and patriotic manner. He said: "At all events I never will consent to let these inventions lie dormant, should my country at any time have need of them. Were you to grant me the annuity of twenty thousand pounds I would sacrifice all to the safety and independence of my country."

Finding that both England and France disapproved of his proposed invention, Mr. Fulton resolved to return to his native land.

Before starting on the voyage to America he made careful drawings and explanations of his boat and torpedo. These he left in England, so that in case of shipwreck, as he said, "the result of my studies and experience may not be lost to my country."

He expected to start in October and arrive at New York in November. He wrote to his friend, Mr. Barlow, who had already gone back to the United States: "I shall be with you I hope, in November, perhaps about the fourteenth, my birthday, so you must have a roast goose ready."

But he spent that birthday at sea. It was the thirteenth of December, 1806, when he landed in New York. He brought with him good health, good spirits, a high reputation, and great hopes. Moreover he had about £15,000, received for past work, many valuable pictures, and, last but not least, a mysterious steam engine.

CHAPTER VI

MAKING THE STEAMBOAT

There was a close connection between Robert Fulton's good spirits and that steam engine.

Do you remember the paddle wheels he made for the old fishing boat on the Conestoga River, when he was a boy? Those wheels were turned by a crank, and the boys had to turn the crank. Robert Fulton had often thought of that boat. How well it went when the crank was turned fast enough! If only an engine could be made for turning the crank, how much better a boat moved by paddle wheels would be than one moved by wind and sails! The steam engine which Mr. Fulton brought from England was intended for that very purpose. And now I will tell you how he got it.

While Mr. Fulton was staying in Paris, Chancellor Robert R. Livingston, a wealthy American patriot and statesman, went to France to act as United States minister to that country. The two men became acquainted.

Mr. Livingston was interested in science and mechanics. He had tried to make a steamboat but had failed. He still believed, however, that a steamboat could be made. Robert Fulton told him that he considered

ROBERT R. LIVINGSTON

the steamboat both a possibility and a necessity. He was surprised that no one who had tried to make such a boat had succeeded, and he had often thought of trying it himself, but he had not had enough money for the undertaking.

Mr. Livingston was eager to have him devote his attention to the subject. He promised to furnish a certain portion of the money needed for the experiment. He also promised to use his influence to secure from the New York legislature the sole right to use steamboats on the waters in the state of New York.

Experimenting with steamboats was expensive. So many had tried and failed that it was difficult to find any one who would risk money on a steamboat venture. Mr. Fulton was a practical man and did not act with blind enthusiasm. He counted the cost first, and if a thing was completely beyond his reach he did not attempt it. Before this he had looked upon the steamboat as something impossible, at least for him. But Mr. Livingston's generosity encouraged him to undertake to make such a boat, and with some hope of success.

In 1802, he went to a little village in France. There he made a small model of a steamboat with side wheels turned by machinery. He tried it on a stream, and it was so successful that he returned to Paris and had a large boat made like it.

When the boat was finished, it was launched on the Seine River. That was early in the spring of 1803. Both Mr. Livingston and Mr. Fulton believed that it would prove to be a success. They determined to make a trial trip, and invite their friends and other influential men to be present on that occasion.

But one morning, as Mr. Fulton was dressing, a boy came to his lodgings to tell him that the boat had sunk. When Mr. Fulton heard this his spirits sank too. For a moment he felt that it was useless to make any further efforts towards inventing a steamboat. He finished dressing in haste, and without stopping to eat breakfast, hurried to the place where the boat had been secured the night before. There was no sign of it.

He found that it was under the water. He soon had men at work trying to raise the wreck. He did not merely stand on the bank and give orders to the laborers. He plunged into the river and worked the hardest of all. He worked all day and far into the night, without food or rest. He did not know that his clothes were wet through and through, that the spring air was cold, or that he had been long without food. He had no thought of himself. His whole mind was bent on saving his boat.

His energy inspired his helpers, and before the next day's sun rose, the fragments of the vessel and its engine were safe on dry land. The inventor examined the wreck and found that the vessel had broken in two in the middle. The framework was light and the machinery was heavy. The rocking of the waves had been too much for the little craft.

The machinery was put together again and a stronger boat was made. In August of the same year some of the distinguished citizens of Paris received cards inviting them to view the first trip of Mr. Fulton's steamboat.

It moved off in fine style, and all were well satisfied except the inventor. The boat did not go fast enough to suit him. But he saw that its speed could be increased by building a stronger engine.

Mr. Livingston was ready to furnish the money for such an engine. Mr. Fulton ordered it made in England. He did not tell what the engine was to be used for but gave careful directions as to how it should be constructed.

It was completed in 1806 and sent to America.

Mr. Livingston had succeeded in getting an act passed by the legislature, giving to him and Mr. Fulton the sole right to use boats propelled by "fire or steam" on the waters of New York state for a term of twenty years. The bill was treated as a joke in the legislature. No one thought twenty years too long a time. One man suggested that the term be extended to one hundred or one thousand years; for all thought it improbable that such boats would ever be used at all.

Mr. Fulton had the boat built at the shipyards of Charles Brown on East River. He devoted most of his time during the winter of 1805 to superintending its construction. While it was being made men often stopped to look at the strange craft. Not knowing the inventor they sometimes talked freely in his presence. What they said was not flattering. They thanked fortune they were not so mad as to put faith and money in such a wild scheme. The steamboat enterprise was commonly called "Fulton's folly."

All the money that Mr. Livingston and Mr. Fulton had agreed to put into it had been spent. Still more was needed. They decided to take a third partner, but no one would join them. Mr. Livingston was unwilling to invest any more of his fortune in the venture, and Mr. Fulton had no money to risk.

It was hard to borrow money when he could offer no better security than an untried steamboat. But Mr. Fulton did not find it impossible. He selected men who were intelligent enough to understand and wealthy enough to risk a few thousand dollars. He went to them and explained his need. They laughed at first and refused to help him. But they were moved by his glowing words and his confidence of success, and when he left them it was usually with the money that he had asked for.

By his efforts the boat was finished and ready for trial late in the summer of 1807. She was named, in honor of Chancellor Livingston's beautiful home, the "Clermont." She was 130 feet long, 16½ feet wide, and 4 feet deep. The wheels were 15 feet in diameter with a two feet dip. The boiler was 20 feet by 7 feet by 18 feet.

The owners of the boat invited their friends to join them in the first trip up the Hudson. Some refused because they were ashamed to have it thought that they had any faith in the boat. Others accepted, fearing that they would have to condole with their hosts in their disappointment rather than rejoice with them at their success.

CHAPTER VII

THE TRIAL VOYAGE

It was a fair morning late in the summer of 1807. One man said to another "The *Clermont* is to start to Albany to-day. Let us go down to the wharf to see the end of Fulton's folly." So a great crowd gathered at the dock.

Among the graceful sailboats on the river they saw an ugly, stout, little vessel with a great ungainly smokestack sending out clouds of black smoke. The ends of the boat were decked over, but the middle was open and the machinery was in plain view. There was a small sail at either end, and the colors were flying gayly.

The boat was not pleasing to look at. Even Chancellor Livingston was forced to admit that it was one of the ugliest crafts he had ever seen. "It looks," said he, "like a backwoods sawmill mounted on a scow and set on fire."

The invited guests were on the decks, and Mr. Fulton was moving about among them trying his best to cheer them up. But they would look sad and hopeless. The

DEPARTURE OF THE CLERMONT ON HER FIRST VOYAGE

coldness of his friends and the jokes and jeers of the spectators were hard to bear.

When the command was given to start, the vessel struck out boldly and the wheels churned the blue water into foam. There was a moment of amazed silence. Then a cheer arose. But the boat stopped, and the cheer also stopped before they had gone far.

Those who were on the boat believed it would never go further. They felt that they were being made fun of by the spectators, and wished they were on land. They took no pains to hide their impatience.

It was a trying moment for Mr. Fulton. He stood on a chair where all could see him and begged them to be patient for thirty minutes. He said that if all was not right by that time, he would give up the trip and land the passengers.

His handsome face, his brilliant eyes, his voice full of feeling and earnestness, aroused the sympathy and respect, if not the hopes, of his friends, and they warmly expressed their willingness to wait an hour if need be.

He hurried down to the engine. He found that the difficulty was a very slight one and easily corrected. In a few minutes the little vessel started again, and this time she kept steadily on her way up the river.

Then a great chorus of cheers arose from the throng on the bank. The men who had come to see the end of "Fulton's folly" waved hats and handkerchiefs, and shouted at the top of their voices in honor of the man who had done what had seemed to them impossible.

The inventor and his guests stood on the deck and returned the salute. They were soon out of hearing, for the little boat made good time.

The party on the boat became a merry one. Smiles and handshakes took the place of frowns and shrugs as they sped along. There were about forty persons present. Talented men and beautiful women, the flower of New York, made up the company.

Mr. Livingston had urged two of his granddaughters to go, telling them it would be something to remember as long as they lived. His cousin, Harriet Livingston, one of the famous beauties of that great family, was also on the boat.

They found Mr. Fulton a delightful host. One of the ladies in the party afterwards wrote to a friend that he was the finest looking man on the *Clermont*. She said,

"That son of a Pennsylvania farmer was a prince among men; as modest as he was great, and as handsome as he was modest. His eyes were glowing with love and genius."

The ride up the Hudson was a pleasant one. The passengers sat on deck in comfortable chairs and watched the stately Palisades disappear from view; admired the restful vales around the Tappan Zee, sleeping in the August haze; and looked with pleasure upon the grander beauty of the Highlands.

They chatted about the places of interest which they passed, and the older men pointed out spots that had been made famous in the Revolution. Then they noticed how fast the boat moved, and laughed over their doubts of its success.

Every little while a small group went below with Mr. Fulton to see the engine and hear him good-naturedly explain for the twentieth time the wonderful machinery. They peeped into the furnace at the blazing fire of pine wood. They watched the great wheels and asked the inventor what made them go.

He showed them that the movement of the piston in the steam cylinder kept the crank in motion. A chain wheel or sprocket wheel was attached to the crank and turned by it. It was connected by an endless chain with another sprocket wheel that was fastened to the axle of the paddle wheel. Thus the great paddle wheels were kept turning by a contrivance not unlike that which turns the rear wheel of a chain bicycle.

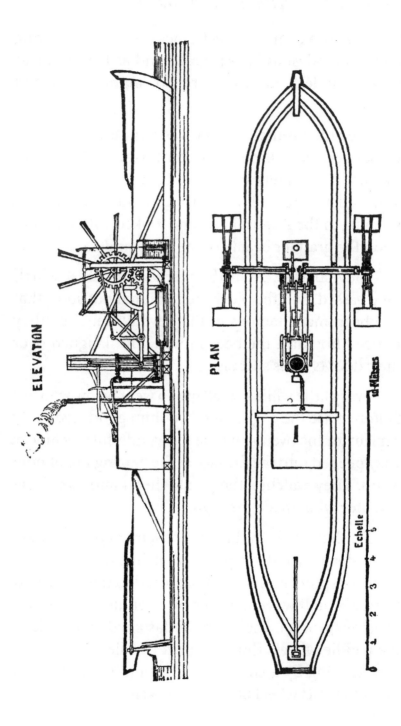

ELEVATION

PLAN

Echelle

PLAN OF FULTON'S FIRST STEAMBOAT, 1803

As the guests began to tire of these things they were called up by a laugh from the party on deck. They arrived just too late to see a company of boys and girls, who had been fishing on the bank, drop their rods and run screaming into the woods to escape from the fiery monster coming up the river.

In the evening the tables were spread on deck and an ample supper was served. After the tables were cleared, beds were made and hammocks were swung. Most of the party went to sleep early that night, tired and happy.

But Robert Fulton was too much excited to sleep. He listened to the throbbing engine and the splashing wheel. He watched the trail of sparks streaming across the sky, and he thought of many things.

CHAPTER VIII

SUCCESS

The next morning the passengers awoke to find themselves far on their journey up the Hudson. Every one pronounced the steamboat a success.

They were to stop at Clermont, the home of Mr. Livingston, to land the guests and give the crew a chance to rest.

A short time before they reached the place the passengers were called together and Chancellor Livingston made a speech. He spoke in glowing terms of Robert Fulton and the great work he had done. Then he announced the betrothal of Robert Fulton and the charming Harriet Livingston.

Many were surprised and all were delighted at this announcement, and Mr. Fulton was overwhelmed with congratulations and good wishes.

The *Clermont* reached Clermont, its namesake, at one o'clock on Tuesday. The journey of one hundred and ten miles had been completed in twenty-four hours. This was better time than the best sailboats ever made, and Mr. Fulton and Mr. Livingston both felt more than satisfied.

Robert R. Livingston lived in grand style. His home was considered the finest house in America. His beautiful park extended for a mile along the Hudson. The mansion was built in the form of the letter H, and each arm of the H was a hundred feet long. The great house was furnished with rare and beautiful furniture brought from France. The sideboards were loaded with heavy dishes of solid silver. In the library there were over six thousand books. The walls were hung with portraits and fine paintings. A large conservatory added to the beauty of the establishment. Everything was in keeping with the luxury of the interior. When the chancellor went out to drive he rode in a gilded coach drawn by four horses. He kept three sets of horses to suit the weather: black ones for bright weather, white ones for cloudy weather, and gray ones for wet weather.

He was a hospitable man, and the old house had been the scene of many a stately gathering. You may be sure the rooms were brilliant with wax-candle lights on the evening after the arrival of the steamboat party, and everything was done to celebrate in grand style the success of the chancellor's pet enterprise. Robert Fulton was the guest of honor. He enjoyed the evening fully and said to himself "This is success. The reward is worth the effort."

The pleasures at Clermont were not strong enough to lure the inventor from his boat, and the next morning at nine o'clock he said farewell to the gay company there and went on up the river with his crew.

That day he sat alone on the deck watching the

steady progress of his vessel. He thought what a great benefit the steamboat would be to mankind. It would make it possible to explore and settle the vast western wildernesses of the United States. The mysteries of the Mississippi and the Missouri would disappear before the steamboat. What cheer the steamboat would carry to the western pioneers, struggling and working bravely so far from their fellow men! It would take them news of the civilized world, letters, friends, and neighbors. When it was perfected, how quickly and safely men could travel from city to city and country to country! Then he said to himself again, "This is success. The reward is worth the effort."

He reached Albany at five o'clock that evening and started back to New York at nine the next morning.

Just as the boat was about to start, a man jumped aboard and asked, "What is the fare to New York?"

Mr. Fulton thought a moment, then said, "Seven dollars."

As he pocketed his first steamboat earnings he smiled brightly and thought, "This, too, is success."

With the exception of an hour's stop at Clermont there was no interruption to his homeward voyage.

It was very amusing to see the excitement caused by the strange-looking bark. Some people stared at her in open-mouthed wonder; others ran away in fear. She caused most alarm at night. Her shrill whistle startled the fishermen, and when they saw the boat plunging towards them with side lights gleaming and a column of smoke and fire rising from the smokestack they thought some monster of the deep was ready to devour them, and fled in terror.

On reaching New York Mr. Fulton reported a trip of one hundred and fifty miles in thirty hours. He heard no more of "Fulton's folly." He found that Mr. Robert Fulton, the inventor of the steamboat, was a man of some importance.

CHAPTER IX

STEAMBOATS ON THE HUDSON

Being satisfied with the *Clermont's* first trip, Mr. Fulton went to work at once to prepare her for a regular passenger boat. He had the machinery decked over and the sides boarded up. He fitted up each of the cabins with twelve berths. Much of the iron work had to be strengthened, too.

By the middle of the following week the boat was ready to start. The fares were the same as those on the regular sail boats. Seven dollars was the full fare from New York to Albany. The *Clermont* had several advantages over other boats. She made better time, and was more regular. Then she was better fitted to accommodate passengers. Travelers on the *Clermont* did not have to provide their own beds, food, and servants, as they did on most other river boats. She usually had as many passengers as she could accommodate.

On the second of October the following notice was published in a New York paper:

"Mr. Fulton's new-invented steamboat, which is fitted up in a neat style for passengers and is intended to run from New York to Albany as a packet, left here this morning with ninety passengers, against a strong head wind. Notwithstanding which it is judged she moved through the waters at the rate of six miles an hour."

The owners of the *Clermont* planned that she should make three trips a week. One week she would run twice to Albany and once to New York, and the next week she would go twice to New York and once to Albany.

But all was not fair sailing. The machinery was by no means perfect. Accidents happened that laid the boat up for repairs. Not all of the accidents were due to faults in the construction of the boat. The new steamboat had many enemies. The owners of sailing vessels did not like to see business taken out of their hands. They wanted to make it appear that the steamboat was a failure. They ran into her and against her, and took off her wheels and injured her in every way they could.

There were so many attempts to harm her that the matter was carried before the state legislature, and an act was passed declaring any intentional injury to the steamboat a crime punishable by fine or imprisonment.

When the river froze over, and navigation stopped for the winter, there were some who said that the *Clermont* would never be used again. They were mistaken however. She was repaired and improved during the winter, and started out in the spring of 1808, a better boat than ever before.

In advertising the steamer a great point was made of her regularity. She left New York every Saturday evening and reached Albany on Sunday night. She left Albany every Wednesday morning at eight o'clock and arrived at New York the next morning.

Bills were printed telling at what time she would pass important places. Those wishing to take the boat were requested to be on the spot an hour before the stated time in case the boat should be ahead of time.

Steamboats have been improved so that the *Clermont* would seem to passengers of to-day small, inconvenient, and slow. Now great, elegant steamers, fitted with every luxury, leave New York every summer morning, and land hundreds of passengers at Albany in the evening.

But in those times the *Clermont* was regarded as a model of comfort and speed. She was very popular. Her owners soon had other boats on the river running between New York and Albany. So many improvements were made that within less than ten years the trip was made in eighteen instead of thirty hours.

Steamboats were also made to run between other places.

Steam ferry-boats were built to run across Hudson River and East River. In describing one of them Mr. Fulton wrote: "The boat crosses the river, which is a mile and a half broad, when it is calm in fifteen minutes; the average time is twenty minutes. She has had in her at one time eight four-wheel carriages, twenty-nine horses, one hundred passengers, and could have taken three hundred more."

Later, other steamboats were made to run on the Sound and on the Mississippi and Ohio rivers.

High prices were charged for passengers and freight, and the boats were well patronized; but the inventors did not become rich.

There were men who claimed to have invented the steamboat before Fulton. Some built boats and put them on waters which the state had given him the sole right to navigate.

He was repeatedly obliged to go into court to have his rights protected. The expense of lawsuits and the enormous cost of building new steamboats used his money about as fast as he made it.

He found that lawsuits and worry take away much of the satisfaction which an inventor derives from his success. Yet he understood what a blessing the steamboat was to men, and never thought that the reward was not worth the cost.

Although he did not neglect other interests, his attention for a long time was given mainly to the perfection of his great invention.

CHAPTER X

OTHER INTERESTS

To supply the ever-increasing demand for steamboats against so many other claimants would have been too great a burden for most men. But Robert Fulton had wonderful energy. He could stem the torrent of opposition as easily as one of his great steamers could make headway against the ocean tides.

He neglected nothing pertaining to the interests of the steamboat company. He made repeated improvements in the machinery for propelling boats. He also increased the comfort and convenience of the vessels in numberless ways. Nothing was so small as to be unworthy of the great inventor's notice. His sharp eyes seemed to see everything.

A story is told that shows how quick he was to observe little things. A man claimed that he had invented a machine which would go for ever without stopping.

The machine was exhibited in New York, and many were willing to give a dollar to see such a marvelous invention. Mr. Fulton showed no interest in it. He said that he knew too much about mechanics to have any faith in perpetual motion. But he was persuaded to go with some friends to see it.

He not only looked at the swaying pendulum and revolving wheels, he listened, as well, to the noise they made. He said to his friends, "Why, that's a crank motion. Don't you hear it? If this machinery made it the sound would be regular. There must be a crank somewhere."

His charges made the man who was showing the machine very angry, and he said they were false. Mr. Fulton answered that if his friends would stand by him he would prove the truth of what he had said. He then broke away part of the framework and discovered a stout string. Following the string the men reached the attic and found an old man sitting there and turning a crank to which the string was fastened.

Many learned men had been so deceived by the fraud as to write long papers trying to explain the working of the machine. The fine ear of the inventor enabled him to explain the mystery very simply and clearly.

In addition to looking closely after steamboat matters, Mr. Fulton found time to keep up his interest in other subjects. Chief among these were canals and torpedo boats.

We have already spoken of the Erie Canal which crosses the state of New York, connecting the Great Lakes with the Hudson River and making it possible to take grain by water from the Minnesota wheat fields to New York. Although the canal was not begun until after

Mr. Fulton's death, he took an active part in planning it. It is claimed by some of his friends that he was the first to suggest building it; at any rate he was one of the canal commissioners and took a prominent part in deciding upon its location and construction.

He still believed that the torpedo was the weaker nation's safeguard against the warships of the stronger one. In 1810 he published a book called "Torpedo War." His text was, "The liberty of the seas will be the happiness of the earth."

He contrived several devices for defensive and offensive warfare. One of his torpedoes was to be anchored in harbors in times of war. When the enemy's vessel struck it, it would explode and destroy the warship. Another was attached to a harpoon which was to be hurled at an approaching ship from a gun. If the harpoon pierced the side of the ship it would hold the torpedo in place until it was exploded by its clockworks. He also made a water-tight gun to be fired under water.

The government gave him little financial encouragement. But he was recognized as an authority on explosives.

During the War of 1812, the people of New York became alarmed lest the British fleet should enter their harbor. They had a public meeting and appointed a committee on coast and harbor defense. This committee went to Mr. Fulton for advice. He recommended a warship to be propelled by steam and armed with forty-four guns.

His plans were approved and he was chosen to construct the first steam warship in the world.

While working on that he was also making plans for a submarine war vessel.

CHAPTER XI

HIS WORK ENDED

It was in the spring of 1814, that Mr. Fulton was commissioned to construct the warship. He was full of enthusiasm. He now had an opportunity to combine the two great forces with which he delighted to work and to show the world what could be done with steam and gunpowder.

Under his vigorous direction the work advanced with astonishing rapidity during the summer and autumn. He loved his work and no difficulty was too great for him to overcome.

Every one was watching the progress of the structure with interest and satisfaction.

In January, Mr. Fulton took a severe cold, but he kept at his work, going about from the shipyards to the foundry on bitter winter days. He was accustomed to inspect the work regularly. He moved among the workmen with a beaming smile for good work, a sharp rebuke for carelessness, a timely word of advice or encouragement where it was needed, and close inspection everywhere.

These visits suddenly stopped, and on the twenty-fourth of February it was announced that Mr. Fulton was dead.

This sad event was a shock to every one. The people of New York felt that they had lost one of their most gifted and distinguished citizens, a public benefactor. The newspapers that announced his death were bordered in black. All spoke of the event with sorrow. Clubs and societies held memorial meetings in his honor. The state legislature at Albany voted that the members should wear mourning badges in his honor for a stated time.

Hundreds of friends, from the dignitaries of the city to the humble mechanic, followed his remains from the Fulton home on State street to Trinity Church; a salute was fired from the Battery, and the flags on all the ships in the harbor were at half-mast. The body was interred in the Livingston tomb in Trinity churchyard.

Mr. Fulton had never filled a public office, and it was said that no other private citizen had been so generally mourned.

The cities and countries of the earth are now joined in peaceful commerce by great railroads and strong steamboats that are driven across the ocean by screw propellers instead of side wheels. The means by which Fulton thought to accomplish the result have been somewhat changed, but the ends he worked for have been accomplished.

THE STORY OF
ELI WHITNEY

ELI WHITNEY

CHAPTER I

CHILDHOOD

If a teacher should ask her pupils to guess where Eli Whitney, the inventor of the cotton gin, was born, the bright-eyed girl who always has her hand up first, would probably answer, "In the South where cotton grows." And the other pupils would think she must be right.

But strange as it may seem there were very few cotton fields in the South when Eli Whitney was born. And his childhood home was far away from them on a New England farm, near the inland village of Westboro, Massachusetts.

There cold weather came early in the fall and lingered until late in the spring. The snow-covered hills and meadows were the only "cotton fields" that little Eli knew anything about.

He was born on a bleak December day in 1765, more than ten years before the signing of the Declaration of Independence.

The Whitney home was one of those plain New England farmhouses that are still common in that part of the country. This two-storied frame dwelling was built near the road. A little "stoop" about five feet long and three feet wide served for a front porch.

But if the porch was small, the chimney was large, and the fireplaces were broad and deep. The narrow mantels above were so high that there was no danger of the children's breaking the plates and candlesticks that ornamented them.

The ceilings were low. The rooms were lighted by wide old-fashioned windows with twelve small panes of glass in each sash. The window-sills were so far from the floor that Eli and his sister had to stand on chairs when they wanted to scratch pictures in the frost which, in winter, often covered the panes in spite of the fires in the big fireplaces.

In the best room there was fine furniture, which had been bought at the shops. But the other rooms were furnished chiefly with homemade tables and chairs. These were neat and strong, and the rooms were comfortable and homelike.

Mrs. Whitney was an invalid, and died while Eli was still a child. The father was a stern, business-like man, who believed that children should be seen and not heard. Eli's brothers were older than he, and therefore his sister, who was nearest his age, was his favorite playmate.

The children had few playthings, but Eli was seldom at a loss for amusement. Although he asked a great many questions, he always asked them for information, and not simply because he wished to say something.

Almost every farmer had some sort of a shop where, in bad weather, he tinkered away at various things and mended whatever was out of order. Mr. Whitney's shop was well fitted with tools, and when not busy on the farm he worked there, making chairs for the house, wheels for his wagons, and many other useful articles.

Eli was very fond of watching his father and older brothers while they were at work, and he soon learned to do many little things himself. As he grew older he liked to work in the shop better than on the farm. He examined all the machinery in the place until he understood it. He wanted to know how it was made, and was not content till he found out.

His father's big silver watch was to him an object of wonder. How could it keep up its steady "tick, tick"? What made the hands move, one so slowly, the other more rapidly?

AN OLD-FASHIONED WATCH

One Sunday, Mr. Whitney went to church and left his watch at home. Eli stole to his room and pried open the back of the watch to see the wheels. That was very interesting for awhile, but the works were partly hidden. One wheel was over another. A little metal plate covered something which he wanted to see.

The curious boy was not long in finding the tiny screws that held all in place. He soon had them out, and took the works apart.

So deeply interested was he that had his father come home then, Eli would not have heard his step, and the stern man might have walked right into the room before the mischief maker discovered his presence.

But fortunately for the lad, church lasted a long time in those days, and he had plenty of time to satisfy his curiosity before the odors from the kitchen warned him that it would soon be dinner time, and his father would be at home.

Then he felt somewhat worried, but he had noticed so closely the relation of each of the members to the others that he was able to put the delicate works together correctly. It was with a deep breath of relief that he heard the familiar tick, and he trembled whenever he saw his father look at the watch that day. But it was uninjured, and not until years later when Eli told him did Mr. Whitney know that it had been meddled with.

Once after an absence of several days Mr. Whitney, on coming home, asked the housekeeper how each of the boys had spent his time while he was away. He learned that one had weeded the onions, and another had mended the stone wall between two fields.

"But what has Eli been doing?" asked the father, noticing that no account was given of him.

"Oh, he has been making a fiddle," she answered.

"Ah," said Mr. Whitney, with a sigh, "I fear Eli will have to take his portion in fiddles."

The fiddle proved to be a very fine piece of work for a twelve-year-old boy. It was made like any other violin and gave fairly good music. Every one that saw it was astonished; and after that all the musicians in the neighborhood brought Eli their violins to mend when they were out of order. He was usually successful in discovering and correcting any faults in their mechanism.

His father, however, looked upon this work as foolishness. He would have been much better pleased to see Eli do a good day's work on the farm.

CHAPTER II

YOUTH

The New England farmers were a very intelligent class of people and understood the value of education. Every settlement had its little school.

Eli Whitney went to the Westboro school, where he studied spelling and learned to read and write. When he began to study arithmetic he made rapid advancement and soon stood at the head of his class. But his pleasantest and most profitable hours were spent in his father's workshop. Every day he grew more fond of working there.

When Eli was thirteen years old his father married a second time. Eli's step-mother took to her new home many choice possessions that she had collected since her girlhood. She liked to look at her treasures and show them to others.

One afternoon she was showing them to Eli and his sister. Among the parcels was a fine set of dinner knives. When she unwrapped them Eli eagerly took one and examined it with a beaming face.

Mrs. Whitney was pleased to see that the boy was

interested. "These are very fine knives," she said. "They were made in England. Nothing like them could be made in this country."

At this Eli looked up quickly and said: "I could make them myself if I had the tools; and I could make the tools if I had some common tools to work with."

Mrs. Whitney was displeased and reproved him. She did not think for a moment that this little boy could do such work, or that he even meant what he said. He seemed to her to be bragging and trying to make fun of her for treasuring those knives.

However, in a few weeks Eli had an opportunity to prove the truth of what he had said. By accident one of the precious knives was broken. He took the pieces to the shop for a model, and with his clumsy tools made a knife so like the broken one that Mrs. Whitney could tell it from the others only by the absence of the stamp of the manufacturer on the blade.

It is needless to say that she now regretted her hasty words. From that time she had much greater confidence in the boy's ability to do what he undertook.

Two years later Eli began to use his skill to make money for his father. His occupation was nail-making.

As the Revolutionary War was then in progress, all trade between England and America had stopped. There were then few manufactories of any kind on this side of the Atlantic. The colonies depended upon the mother country even for such little things as nails.

Nails were made by hand and were much more expensive than they are now. Eli Whitney had often made small quantities of nails for family use, and he had done it very quickly and well. Now that they were so scarce it seemed to him that there would be profit in making them to sell. He spoke to his father about it, saying that he felt sure he could make the work pay if he had certain tools.

The idea pleased his father and he bought the necessary outfit at once. From that time till the close of the war the young mechanic spent all the time he could spare from farm labor in making nails. It proved such a profitable employment that he enlarged his shop and took an assistant.

After the war was over, nails were again shipped to this country and sold for less than young Whitney could afford to make them. He saw that it was useless to try to work against the great nail makers of England.

HAND-MADE
NAILS

But he would not think of letting his shop lie idle. He turned it into a factory for the making of walking sticks and hat pins. He was as successful in manufacturing these little articles as he had been in making nails. He was careless in nothing, and often said, "Whatever is worth doing at all, is worth doing well."

Mr. Whitney had long ceased to regret Eli's fondness for tinkering about the shop. He now expected him to settle down and become a contented, self-supporting mechanic.

But Eli was not satisfied to do this. As he grew older he took more interest in books. In one way or another he had picked up a great deal of general information, and had acquired a surprising amount of useful knowledge. He saw that those who succeeded in life were educated men; and he was ambitious to be more than a common day laborer.

Accordingly, when he was nineteen years old he decided to go to Yale College and get a thorough education.

His father was surprised and somewhat pleased at the idea of having one of his sons go to college. But when the good man spoke to his wife about it she firmly opposed the project. She said that Eli had neither the money nor the knowledge to go to college, and advised him not to think of it, as it would only make him discontented and restless. She told him that since he was already making a good living he ought to be satisfied.

The neighbors agreed with her, and said it would be too bad to spoil such a good mechanic by sending him to college.

The young man now understood that he would get no help from his family. What his stepmother had said was only too true: he had neither the knowledge required to enter Yale College, nor the money that would be required to support him while studying there. But he was not easily discouraged. When he made up his mind to do anything he usually accomplished it.

He said no more about the matter but worked early and late to secure the two things needful. To prepare himself for the entrance examinations he took his books to the shop and studied while his fingers did the work for which they had been trained. He made friends with educated people wherever he could, and got all the hints and helps possible.

Nor was he less zealous to get money. Farm work, shop work, and school teaching occupied his time. He welcomed any task whereby he could earn something to add to the little store he was saving for his education.

Although he was so industrious he was twenty-three years old before he was ready to start to college. For four years the plucky fellow had made a brave struggle against many difficulties, with no encouragement except from his faithful sister.

And now that he was ready and could say proudly, "Next May I shall enter Yale College," an unexpected misfortune threatened to disappoint his hopes.

He was taken ill and suffered for weeks from a severe fever. For a time his life was in danger. But, the fever having finally been broken, he slowly gained strength and in May he was able to go to college as he had hoped.

CHAPTER III

AT YALE

Every fall hundreds of boys who have just finished high school go from all parts of the country to New Haven, to enter Yale College.

Some arrive on the big steamboats. Others come in on the great railroads over which well-filled trains fly back and forth, to and from Boston and New York.

These students find New Haven a large city. Many noisy factories are there. The broad avenues are bordered by beautiful homes, large business blocks, and other fine buildings. Noble elms grow along the streets. Electric cars, and wagons, and carriages of all kinds rumble over the pavements.

In the heart of this busy city is a great square called the Green, where three historic churches stand.

Just beyond the Green rises a row of fine buildings of brick and stone. These are some of the university buildings. They are so stately that they make the stores near by look small and common.

Passing through a broad arch or gateway, the student finds himself within the Yale yard, or campus. It is a large pleasant quadrangle where elms wave overhead, while their lacy shadows dance on the sunny grass. Boys and young men hurry up and down the long walks with armloads of books.

This quadrangle is shut in by four rows of lofty college buildings. A line of plain, old-fashioned brick halls extends across it. These buildings are so poor and old that they look out of place beside the handsome new ones around them.

When Eli Whitney looked out of the windows of the stage coach that took him to New Haven he saw only a straggling village. At that time only about four thousand people lived in New Haven. But it seemed a large town to the young man from Westboro. He had never dreamed of such elegant structures as Osborn and Vanderbilt Halls; and the plain brick buildings, which look to us poor and common, were so much better than the neighboring shops that they appeared grand and stately.

When young Whitney went up to take his examinations, he looked with almost a feeling of reverence at the Old Chapel, the Old South, and the Old South Middle, as the buildings are called.

He passed his examinations and entered the first or freshman class.

There are now almost as many teachers at Yale as there were students then. At that time the president and two or three assistants gave all of the instruction. The president had charge of the advanced classes. The lower classes were taught by young tutors.

President Stiles was a very scholarly man. The students were expected to treat him with the highest respect, and they really stood in great awe of him. When he entered the chapel all rose and remained standing while he walked down the aisle bowing with gracious dignity to the right and to the left.

If a boy went to the president's house to see him on some school business, no matter how cold it was, he took his hat off at the gate and kept it off until he left the yard again.

Though the tutors were young men who had not been out of school very long themselves, they were treated with almost as high regard as the president.

The seniors had great power over the lower classes. Shortly after school opened each year there was a meeting of the freshman and senior classes. The freshmen formed a line along one side of the long hall and the seniors lined up along the opposite side. Then the gravest and most dignified member of the senior class stepped forward and gave the freshmen a lecture on college rules and manners.

The younger students were expected to obey all the orders of the seniors, and were punished severely by them for disrespectful behavior.

It would have been very hard for Mr. Whitney, who was then twenty-three years old, to submit to the tyranny of the youths of the upper classes. But he had very little to do with them. He found that he could get board in a private family for much less than it would cost him to live at the college halls, and he took advantage of that chance to save his money.

During the first year he studied Latin, the Greek Testament, and arithmetic. He had the power to put his whole mind on one subject and keep it there as long as he wanted to, and therefore it did not take him long to get his lessons.

He found that he would have some extra time for work. A carpenter was working at the house where he boarded. Mr. Whitney asked if he might use his tools. The man was afraid the college student would injure them, and refused to let him take them. The owner of the house heard the conversation. He had formed so high an opinion of his boarder that he asked the man to lend him his tools, saying that he would pay for whatever was broken.

The carpenter gave his consent, but watched critically while the college man began to work. He was so astonished when he saw how adroitly he handled every tool, that he exclaimed, "There was one good mechanic spoiled when you went to college." After that Mr. Whitney was permitted to use the tools whenever he liked.

Thus by doing occasional odd jobs, and by working during vacations, he was able to continue at college for the entire course.

As he went into higher classes, he had to spend more time in study. In the second year he took geography, grammar, rhetoric, algebra, geometry, and the catechism, in addition to Greek and Latin. The teachers were very exacting, and required the pupils to learn their lessons word for word. Some of the text books were dry and uninteresting.

In the third or junior year young Whitney commenced the study of trigonometry and philosophy. He liked both of those subjects very much.

It was with keen pleasure that he went to his recitations in natural philosophy. They were held on the second floor of the Old College, in a corner room where the shutters were usually mysteriously closed. There all of the delicate instruments belonging to the college were kept. A telescope, an air-pump, a magic lantern, and an electrical machine were among its treasures.

One day the teacher of this class said that he was unable to make a certain experiment because his instrument was broken. He added that it would be necessary to send it to Europe to have it put in order, as there were no mechanics in this country skillful enough to mend it.

Eli Whitney looked at it for a moment, and then said, "I see just what is the matter, and I think there is no reason why I cannot mend it."

Although the teacher had great confidence in his student, he was surprised at this offer and scarcely willing to trust such a valuable instrument to him. However, when Mr. Whitney explained to him what would have to be done, and assured him that he could do it, he consented to let him try. The clever workman put it in perfect order, to the surprise and delight of both teacher and classmates.

71

By that time he had begun to take a more active part in college life. He was known and liked by the students of all classes, and was a prominent member of one of the literary societies.

He made life-long friendships at college with men who were to be the social and political leaders of their time. And he graduated with credit in the spring of 1792.

CHAPTER IV

IN GEORGIA

Having finished college, Mr. Whitney wished to study law and become a lawyer. He had spent all his own money and had even borrowed some from his father to finish his course at Yale. It would therefore be necessary for him to earn more before he could go on with his study.

While he was looking about for something to do, he was offered a position as teacher in a small private school in Georgia. He had had some experience in teaching. Then, too, it would be very pleasant and instructive to spend a winter in the South. So he accepted the position.

It was a hard journey over land from New Haven to Georgia; for in those days there were no railroads, and only very poor wagon roads. For this reason the young traveler embarked on one of the slow boats and went by sea.

He was not alone on his voyage. At New York he met Mrs. Greene and her children who were on their way to their beautiful southern home at Mulberry Grove, a few miles from Savannah. Mrs. Greene was the widow of the great General Nathanael Greene whose victories in the South are remembered by every schoolboy that has read the history of the Revolution.

Mrs. Greene was a brilliant little woman. She was admired and loved by George and Martha Washington, and accustomed to the gayest and most elegant society in the land. Perhaps it was because her famous husband had been so deeply interested in young men who had gone through college and were trying to make something of their lives, that she took such an interest in the young New England school teacher and mechanic.

She was very kind to Mr. Whitney and made him feel quite at home in her party. It pleased her to see her boys and girls fond of him. They had not been together many days before she had made up her mind that Eli Whitney was no ordinary young man.

When he reached Savannah Mr. Whitney found that the position he had come to fill was not as had been represented to him. The salary was only half as large as he had expected. This was a great disappointment.

On hearing of his trouble, Mrs. Greene said, "Do not think of taking the position. Come to my home and wait till a better opportunity offers. In the meantime you can study law. You will be very welcome. It will be a great pleasure to us to have you with us for a few weeks."

Her children, who were delighted at the idea of having their new friend at their home, added their affectionate entreaties to their mother's invitation. So he was persuaded to visit Mulberry Grove, although

GENERAL NATHANAEL GREENE

he hesitated to refuse the school, and still thought of taking it if he could get nothing better.

He found Mulberry Grove to be a beautiful estate situated on the Savannah River, about fourteen miles from the city of Savannah.

The house was large and magnificent, and furnished with all possible luxury and elegance; for it had been the home of the Tory governor of Georgia in the days before the Revolution. To Mr. Whitney, one of the most attractive features of the house, was the large, well-stocked library.

Around the house was a beautiful garden where all sorts of flowers and fruits grew in abundance. Peaches, apricots, figs, oranges, and plums were in various stages of perfection. The whistle of the mocking bird in the magnolia trees trilled through the warm air.

In the rear of the mansion was the large kitchen, in a separate building. Beyond that were the smokehouse, the coach house, the stables, and the poultry pens fitted for the accommodation of thousands of fowls.

In the distance extended vast corn and rice fields, where the negroes in gay garments were at work planting, cultivating, or harvesting.

Mr. Whitney was much interested in the great plantation. Such luxury was surprising to one brought up as he had been. Even at that time there was a strong spirit against slavery in some parts of New England. The visitor at Mulberry Grove shared that feeling, and observed the plantation slaves with great interest and sympathy. He learned that they were much afraid of the smallpox, and shortly after his arrival he vaccinated all of them.

Mr. Whitney tried in every way possible to show his appreciation of the kindness of his hostess. If anything was out of order in the house or on the plantation he seemed to know exactly what was needed to make it right.

One day he heard Mrs. Greene complain that her embroidery frame tore the threads of the delicate cloth she was embroidering. He looked at it and pronounced it a clumsy contrivance. He left the room, and soon came back with a very different frame exactly suited to the purpose.

"Where did you get it?" asked Mrs. Greene.

"I made it," he replied, helping her to adjust the work on the new frame.

"But it is such a fine idea," she went on enthusiastically. "Where did you get the idea?"

"Oh, I made that too," he answered, laughing.

CHAPTER V

THE OPPORTUNITY

Mrs. Greene was a woman of much importance and had great social influence. She was acquainted with the most prominent families in the country, and was very popular. In the dark days of the war, her husband said that whenever the news reached camp that she was coming to make him a visit, the whole camp was glad. While enjoying one of those happy visits the great soldier wrote to a friend: "Her cheerful countenance and ready tongue quite triumph over my grave face."

Now that the bright little northern lady had come to make her home in the South, old army officers and neighboring planters frequently stopped, on their way to and from Savannah, to have a visit at Mulberry Grove.

One afternoon, when a large party of officers and plantation owners from the neighborhood of Augusta were at the plantation, the conversation was about the discouraging state of affairs in the South, the heavy debt, and the number of people that were going west. One said, "If we could only find a way to separate rapidly the short-staple cotton from the seed it would bring new life to the South." The others agreed that this was so.

"Now," thought Mrs. Greene, "is the time to interest these influential men in my poor young friend, Mr. Whitney." Then she said, "Gentlemen, I have a friend who has just come from the North, a graduate of Yale College. He is a perfect genius at contriving machinery. Indeed, it seems to me he can make anything. Explain to him what is wanted, and I am sure he can help you."

Then she showed them her embroidery frame, and explained its good points, while a servant went to call the young man.

Mr. Whitney was in his room studying hard in a great law book, not thinking of the beautiful country around him, or of its products, when the polite servant summoned him to go below to meet some gentlemen.

"Perhaps they are lawyers. This may be an opportunity," he thought to himself as he hurried down stairs.

He listened eagerly to what the gentlemen said, and learned a great deal about cotton. He became much interested in the subject, and promised to see what he could do.

In those days tobacco and indigo were the chief products of the inland plantations. Large quantities of rice and some cotton were raised near the coast.

There are two kinds of cotton that may be compared just as we compare two varieties of peaches. You know that, while all peaches are very much alike, there are two kinds, the freestone peach from which the stone is easily removed, and the clingstone peach whose stone and pulp adhere so closely that it is almost impossible to separate them.

SEA-ISLAND COTTON

It is so with cotton. There is one black-seed, long-staple variety, that is called sea-island cotton, since it grows well only near salt water. The seeds of this cotton are removed with little difficulty. Then there is the green-seed, short-staple cotton which can be raised on inland plantations. The fiber and seeds cling to each other so closely that it is hard work to get them apart.

GREEN-SEED COTTON

For years the planters along the coast had raised enough of the first kind for family use. A rude machine, called a roller gin, was used for separating this cotton wool from the seeds. It consisted of two wooden rollers which turned towards each other and acted on the same principle as the common clothes-wringer. The staple passed between these rollers, and the seeds were either squeezed back or crushed in passing through, just as you have seen buttons treated by a wringer.

Recently large crops of short-staple, green-seed

cotton had been raised successfully on the high land. The climate and soil of the upper country, where rice could not be cultivated, were well suited to the growth of this cotton.

Improvements in the method of spinning and weaving had made a great demand for cotton, and the planters of the upper country wished to turn their tobacco fields into cotton fields. But after the cotton was raised there was no machine to separate the seeds from the fiber. The roller gin could not be used with this kind of cotton, and the separating had to be done by hand.

It was a day's work for a woman to pick the seeds from a pound of cotton, and the women servants were needed for other work.

THE OLD WAY OF CLEANING COTTON

It was customary on the plantations where cotton was raised to require the slaves to spend their evenings cleaning it. Men, women, and children sat in circles working by the light of tallow candles. Sometimes they sat quiet and sullen at their work. Sometimes they sang plantation songs, or told stories, or made rude jokes and laughed heartily, showing gleaming rows of white teeth. But, whatever expression the dark faces, bent over the snowy cotton, wore, the fingers worked busily, for there was an overseer close at hand to see that there was no idleness.

Every family of slaves was expected to separate about four and a half pounds in a week in addition to doing the field work. The slaves did not like it, and their masters were little better satisfied. At best, it was slow work, and the planters were anxious to find an improved method for removing the seeds.

Not many days passed before some of Mrs. Greene's friends came back to see what progress the Northerner had made in solving the problem. Eli Whitney had not been idle.

He had never seen cotton in the seed, and as there was none to be had at Mulberry Grove, he had gone to Savannah to get some.

He had experimented a little with it, and had formed a rough plan for a machine. He said that he had thought the matter over carefully and did not doubt that he could make a machine to do the work. But it would be an expensive undertaking, and would so interrupt his law studies that he could not afford to go into it.

His hearers assured him that in case he succeeded he was sure to make a fortune. But he still shook his head. Success was doubtful, he said, even if he made a good model. Others would use his invention before he could get money to make his machines and put them on the market.

They reminded him of the patent laws designed to protect inventors and prevent others from using their ideas without permission. He still hesitated, saying that it would be hard to enforce those laws.

The truth was, he had no money to spend in making the experiment. Gradually the disappointed planters stopped urging and went away. Mr. Miller, the man who had charge of Mrs. Greene's estate, stayed. He had talked much with Mr. Whitney and had heard him explain his plan.

When all the others had gone, he said, "Mr. Whitney I believe you can do this, and if you will undertake it I will become your partner. I will furnish all the money necessary until you get the patent, on condition that I receive half the profits when we begin work."

Mr. Whitney gladly accepted this generous offer.

CHAPTER VI

MAKING THE COTTON GIN

The important question of "Who will pay for the venture?" having been settled, Mr. Whitney devoted his attention to the still greater one, "How may cotton be separated from the seed?"

He had formed a rough plan for a machine which he thought would answer the question satisfactorily. The next thing in order was to test his plan by making the machine and trying it.

Mrs. Greene and Mr. Miller had high hopes of his success and were almost as anxious as he to see a cotton gin actually made and at work. Mrs. Greene had a shop fitted up in the basement, where the inventor worked behind locked doors.

Her children were surprised to find themselves refused admission by their accommodating friend. They became very curious to know what was going on in the mysterious room. But the inventor met all their questions and jests with easy good nature, and let no one but his hostess and Mr. Miller into the secret.

He worked under great disadvantages, for he lacked

many necessary materials which were not to be bought even at Savannah. And it required almost as much ingenuity to carry out his plan as it had taken to make it.

His idea was to mount a cylinder on a strong frame, so that it could be turned by hand, or by horse or water power. The cylinder was to be provided with rows of teeth, which passed through narrow openings in a curved plate or grating of metal. The rows of teeth, or circular saws, were to be about three fourths of an inch apart. The cotton was to be put into a box, or hopper, so that it rested against the grating through which the saw teeth protruded. When the cylinder was turned, its sharp teeth would catch the cotton and drag it through the grating, tearing it from the seeds and dropping it on the other side, soft and clean. The seeds, which had been left behind, would fall to the bottom of the hopper and pass out through an opening just large enough to let them pass. They would be uninjured by the process, and ready to be planted for another cotton crop.

Mr. Whitney worked rapidly in spite of many inconveniences. But when all was done except the cylinder, progress stopped for a time. His idea had been to make circular saws and mount them one after the other on the cylinder. To make them, he must have tin or steel plates. As he could not buy or make such plates, he was obliged to contrive some other way of making the teeth on the cylinder.

One day as he was sitting in the quiet parlor, trying to think of something to use in place of the saws, one of

Mrs. Greene's daughters came in with a coil of strong wire in her hand.

"I have caught you at last! Won't you help me make a bird cage?" she coaxed, holding out the wire with a bright smile.

A SMALL COTTON GIN

Mr. Whitney was always glad to use his quick wits and nimble fingers to please his little friends. But never had he performed a task more cheerfully than this; for the little maid had brought him a suggestion with her request.

With a light heart he returned to his shop and was soon busy cutting pieces of wire into required lengths.

Soon the clever workman had a wooden cylinder, armed with rings of wire teeth, mounted and ready for use.

What an exciting moment it was when he put the cotton into the hopper and his hand on the crank! How much the result meant to the man! With glowing cheeks and bated breath, he watched the cylinder turn and the wire teeth carry through the openings of the plate a burden of snowy cotton free from seeds.

That was a moment of victory. Past years of toil and patient striving were forgotten. Visions of comfort, luxury, and honor, thoughts of his father's and friends' surprise and pleasure, filled his mind for a moment.

Then he dismissed those dreams and studied the working of the machine more closely. He saw that the cotton lint clogged the teeth of the cylinder. There were many little improvements that must be made before the gin was perfect. But the main object was accomplished. He had made a machine that would separate cotton from the seed.

In high spirits he called his friends to share his triumph. Both were delighted. "I knew you could do it," said Mrs. Greene, with tears of pleasure in her eyes.

Mr. Miller was no less enthusiastic. "Our fortune is made, man! You've invented a gold mine!" he exclaimed, bending over to examine the wonderful gin.

The inventor tried to check their ardor by saying that the work was by no means finished. "We must find a way to get the cotton off the teeth," he said, turning the crank slowly and plucking at the stubborn lint.

"That is only a trifle," answered Mrs. Greene gayly. Then she picked up the hearth brush and asked with a light laugh, "Why don't you use that?"

"Thank you, I will," he said, taking the offered brush and trying it. "And now I must get to work again."

Again the doors were locked, and when the confidants were next admitted, they saw a second cylinder that turned towards the first one. It had rows of little brushes which met the wire teeth and swept the cotton off of them as the two cylinders revolved.

Mrs. Greene wanted to celebrate her friend's success. She invited leading men from all parts of the state to come to Mulberry Grove to see the gin in operation.

A booth was built in the garden and decorated with flowers and foliage. There the gin was exhibited. The planters stood around it and watched with wonder and admiration, while it did in a few minutes as much as had hitherto been called a day's work.

That was a great day, and Eli Whitney was the hero of it. Every one praised and congratulated him. They called him the benefactor of the South. He was in high spirits and answered without reserve the many questions asked by the planters. He talked of the difficulties he had had to overcome in making the model. Among other things, he told how he had first thought of using metal sheets instead of wire to make the teeth of the cylinder.

A new future seemed in store for the South. In fancy the planters saw endless cotton fields sweeping over hill and plain. All decided to plant their rich acres in cotton the next season.

Their astonishment and satisfaction were so great that they could not restrain their feelings. They talked about the wonderful invention everywhere. As the news spread, crowds of curious people visited Mulberry Grove to see the inventor and his marvelous machine.

But Mr. Whitney had not yet obtained a patent on his machine. That is, he had not gotten from the government the right to control the manufacture and use, or sale, of the cotton gin. It was therefore thought best not to show it to many, lest some one should steal the idea and get a patent before Mr. Whitney did. Hence many visitors went away disappointed.

The excitement about it was so great that the gin was not safe. It was kept constantly under lock and key. One night, in spite of that care, some men broke into the shed where the precious machine was kept and took it away.

With all haste possible, Mr. Whitney made another model and sent it to the patent office at Philadelphia, which was then the seat of the national government.

CHAPTER VII

GREAT EXPECTATIONS

Papers were made out, formally organizing the firm of Miller & Whitney. At first the two men thought that they would manufacture cotton gins and sell them to planters, or sell the right to manufacture to those who wanted to make gins.

But they decided that it would be more profitable to do the ginning themselves and take their pay in cotton. The planters were willing to give them, in payment for their work, one out of every three pounds of cotton they ginned.

To handle the entire cotton crop of the South would be an enormous undertaking. But these two ambitious young men had not the slightest doubt of their ability to do it successfully. They would need a large number of gins, for cotton was being planted in all parts of the South, and the crop promised to be a heavy one.

It was agreed that Mr. Miller should make the terms and the contracts with the planters and look after the company's interests in the South, while Mr. Whitney started a factory and got the gins ready for fall work.

The latter had found by experience that there were no advantages in the South for manufacturing. It would be necessary to make the machines in the North and ship them to Georgia. He felt more at home in his college town, New Haven, than in any other northern city. He knew the shipping advantages there; he knew where he could get supplies; he even knew good workmen whom he could employ. Besides, it was the place he preferred for his future home.

In the spring of 1793 he started north. He went first to the capital to take the proper steps to secure his patent. Thomas Jefferson was then Secretary of State. He was interested in the invention, and said he should like to have one for his own use.

Mr. Whitney stayed at Philadelphia no longer than was necessary and then hastened to New Haven. He had many friends there who were glad to see him back; but he was too busy to find much enjoyment in their company. He did not even take time to visit his father's home at Westboro as he had hoped to do.

Every letter he received from his partner urged him to push the work, and warned him that there would be a great demand for cotton gins.

Mr. Whitney worked early and late, getting his shop ready, training his workmen, and providing proper tools.

As soon as the first machine was completed he went south with it, to see it set up and put in operation. The progress of the enterprise depended largely on the satisfaction given by the first gin; for on its success depended his ability to borrow money to pay for making others.

The result was all that could be desired. Everything promised the most glowing success. The only difficulty would be to make gins fast enough.

To enlarge the factory and push the work the company needed a little more money than they had. Many were ready to lend to such a promising firm as Miller & Whitney, and a loan of two thousand dollars was secured without difficulty.

Mr. Whitney went back to New Haven where he managed the building of an addition to his shop, and employed a large force of workmen.

His intention was to go to England just as soon as he got his affairs in working order. It was important that he should go there without delay, to get a patent in that country. But he was true to his old motto, "Whatever is worth doing at all is worth doing well," and slighted nothing in his hurry.

He took the greatest pains to plan every detail of the factory, so that the work could be most quickly and economically done.

His work was delayed by his own illness and that of his workmen. But in spite of such hindrances he had his shop in the best of order when, at the close of the winter of 1795, he went to New York to attend to a few business affairs before leaving for England.

He had been for two years a very busy, hardworking

man, but a very hopeful one. All was going well, and the future was bright with promise.

CHAPTER VIII

MISFORTUNES

After a short stay in New York Mr. Whitney returned to New Haven. It was a chill March day when he stepped off the boat at the New Haven dock. One of his friends came out of the crowd to greet him.

"You have hard luck, Mr. Whitney," said the man, taking his hand.

"Why, what's the matter?" asked Mr. Whitney, startled by the grave face of his friend.

"You have been burned out," answered the other.

With a look almost of despair the unfortunate man cried, "Is everything gone?" and seeing the other nod his head sadly, he added, "This is indeed a misfortune," and strode off with such long steps that his friend could scarcely keep pace with him.

Arriving at the scene of the fire he found, in place of his well-ordered shop, a desolate ruin. Valuable papers, twenty finished gins, machinery, and shop were all gone. The results of two years of untiring work lay in ashes.

In every letter, Mr. Miller wrote, "We must have a

hundred gins by fall." Those words came to Mr. Whitney at this moment, and he felt helpless and crushed.

But he soon regained his self-control and inquired how the fire had started. He could find out nothing satisfactory about its cause.

Everything had been done in the usual neat and orderly fashion. The night before, the shop had been swept "as clean as a dwelling house." There was not a "hat crown of fire in both chimneys, and not a pailful of chips or shavings in the entire building." The men left the building to go to breakfast. They had been gone not more than ten or fifteen minutes before the whole building was in flames. When the alarm was given, every workman hurried back, pail in hand, to put out the fire. But they saved only the adjoining building and that with the greatest effort.

As the hearths had just been swept, it was Mr. Whitney's opinion that the fire must have started from one of the brooms used for that purpose. But no one ever knew certainly the cause of the fire.

To repair the loss it was necessary for the firm of Miller & Whitney, to borrow more money. It was not so easy that time, and they had to pay a very high rate of interest for it.

Mr. Whitney received word that two other gins, made after the same plan as his own, but changed slightly, were being used in Georgia. The planters would have gins. They were willing to use Miller & Whitney's; but if they could not have them, they would have others.

The trip to England had to be given up. Mr. Whitney used every effort to get the works started again and make up for lost time.

While he was working with might and main to repair the losses he had suffered, another misfortune befell him which was perhaps the heaviest blow of all. It was hard to be hurried and to have more gins needed than he could supply. But there was something even harder than that possible. That was to have planters cease to want the gins.

It never occurred to Mr. Whitney that this was possible, yet it was exactly what happened. It came about in this way: A large quantity of poor cotton was ginned in one of the Whitney gins. It was full of knots. The merchants to whom it was sold returned it. Then some ignorant or wicked person said the fault was due to the Whitney gin.

Thus the report that the famous Whitney gin injured cotton and made it knotty was started. It was generally believed, and spread even to London, so that buyers refused to take cotton that had been ginned by the Whitney machine. And those gins which were already set up in the South stood idle.

At first Mr. Whitney could scarcely take the matter seriously. He could not believe that intelligent men would be influenced by a charge so groundless and unreasonable. Some of the cotton that had been returned was sent to him. He examined it and said: "Nature and not our gin put those knots in the cotton. They would have been in it had it been ginned by hand. As for the gin, it is impossible for it to make such knots in good cotton, as any one may see by trying it."

He soon found that, however unreasonable the report was, it had so influenced the merchants, manufacturers, and planters that they would have nothing to do with the Whitney gin.

The company had had thirty gins at work in Georgia. Some were worked by horses or oxen, and some by water power. One after another they stopped work. Ten thousand dollars had been invested in land to be used for ginning. That was idle and unused.

Mr. Whitney now thought that if he could go to England he might do much to overcome the prejudice against his gin among those who bought and sold cotton. For he knew that if these people could be persuaded to have faith in the gin, the planters would be willing to use it. The trip would cost him one thousand dollars. Neither he nor his partner could furnish so much money, and he was obliged to stay at home and trust to time to cure men of their false notion.

He did what he could at home to show the world that the charge against his gin was unjust. He had seed cotton sent to New Haven where he ginned it to the satisfaction of every one. Samples were widely distributed. An agent was sent out through the Carolinas, and even across the mountains to Tennessee, to investigate the cotton industry and introduce the Whitney gin.

The prejudice against the gin gradually died out. But in the meantime a patent had been granted to a Georgia man on what he called an "improved gin."

While Whitney's gin had been lying idle his had been gaining in popularity.

The new gin was a saw gin. It was like the Whitney gin, but instead of making the teeth for the cylinder of wire, the "improver" had used sheets of metal, as Mr. Whitney had first thought of doing. The machine was Whitney's and the so-called improvement was his idea.

CHAPTER IX

IN THE COURTS

Mr. Whitney had always, even in childhood, a keen sense of justice. He was not the man to stand back and quietly allow another to take what rightfully belonged to him.

He saw that if steps were not taken at once against this man, innumerable modifications of the Whitney gin would spring up and take the place of the original one.

If he had been an uneducated man he would not have known what to do, and this would probably have been the end of his name in connection with the cotton gin. But both he and his partner were men of intelligence. He knew something of law, and he understood mechanics so thoroughly that he was not to be deceived by apparent resemblances or differences in other machines.

In order to encourage ingenious men to give their time and attention to improving machinery and inventing useful articles, the government issues patent rights to inventors who apply for them.

In Whitney's time a patent gave an inventor the exclusive right to make and use or sell his own invention for a term of fourteen years. It was his property, and he might sell or grant to others all or a portion of that right. But for any one to make and use or sell his machine without having received the right to do so from the inventor, was a legal offense. He who did it was said to *infringe* on the rights of the inventor, and was liable to be fined or otherwise punished.

Mr. Whitney had decided to make and use his own gins, and he was determined to punish all who infringed upon his right.

His first suit was brought against Holmes, the man who had made the saw teeth of metal plate instead of wire. Though it was proved that the idea was Whitney's there was a defect in the patent law that made it impossible for Miller & Whitney to win the case.

The law said that the accused had to be guilty of *making, devising, and using, or selling.* The company could only prove that this man had used, not that he had made the gin.

This decision against Whitney encouraged other infringments on his patent. Men with gins which they claimed as their own inventions appeared in all parts of Georgia offering to gin cotton much below the prices asked by Miller & Whitney.

The planters of Georgia were therefore glad to see the true inventor of the cotton gin defeated. There grew up a bitter feeling against him, and it seemed impossible for him to find justice in the courts of Georgia.

He wrote to a friend, "If taking my life would have done away with my claim, I should have had a rifle ball through me long before this time."

Even those who sympathized with him scarcely dared to go into court and tell the truth.

Once, when his attorneys were trying to prove that the cotton gin had been used in Georgia, they had hard work to find any one who would say so, though at the time there were three gins at work so near that the noise of their wheels could be heard from the courthouse steps.

One suit after another was decided against the inventor. Most men would have given up in despair, but Mr. Whitney had a will like iron. He believed two things: that his invention was a good one, and that truth would win in the end.

And at last, after more than sixty trials, which cost him almost as much as he made out of the cotton gin, he came out victorious and proved the claims of his enemies to be false.

The difference in the cylinder teeth had been one of the chief points of dispute. A man claimed to have invented a different gin because he used saws instead of wire teeth. Mr. Whitney was able to show with the help of trustworthy witnesses that the idea of making the teeth in that manner started with him. He further showed that the principle of the gin was the same whether the teeth were made of wire or on steel plates. To make this point so clear that the most ignorant man on the jury would be convinced, he prepared two cylinders, one with saw teeth and the other with wire teeth. In one he buried the saws in the cylinder so that only the long, sharp teeth could be seen. In the other he attached the wire teeth to steel plates. When the witnesses came up to swear which one was the invention of Whitney and which the invention of Holmes, they pointed out the wrong one in each case.

At the end of the long struggle all just men were satisfied that Eli Whitney was the first and only inventor of the cotton gin.

The question was not settled, however, until a year before the close of the fourteen years covered by the patent. So, as far as money was concerned, it was of small benefit to him. Some years before, the company had sold to the states of North Carolina, South Carolina, and Tennessee the right of manufacture within state limits. From these sales Mr. Whitney and his partner received enough to pay for the lawsuits in Georgia, and had a few thousand dollars left.

Towards the close of the struggle Mr. Whitney had realized that he could not depend on lawyers, friends, or assistants of any kind for success. He saw that whatever was gained must be gained through his own efforts. As his business was extended over a wide territory, he had to do a great deal of traveling. In going from New Haven to Savannah he often rode overland in a little two-wheeled cart. The roads were very poor. There were few stopping-places, and those journeys required great exertion and exposure.

He wrote to a friend about these frequent trips

saying, "I am perpetually on the wing and, wild-goose-like, spend my summers in the North, and at the approach of winter, shape my course for the regions of the South. But I am an unfortunate goose. Instead of winging through the airy heights with a select company of faithful companions, I must slowly wade through mud and dirt, a solitary traveler."

The cotton gin cost its inventor thirteen of the best years of his life. He gave to it his splendid business ability and his rare genius. In return he received a little more than enough to pay his debts, fame on two continents, and the knowledge that he had multiplied the riches of southern planters, and that he deserved the gratitude of every man, woman and child, who sleeps snugly under a soft cotton-filled comfort on a winter night, or who wears a cool cotton garment on a summer day.

An effort was made to lengthen the term of the patent. But men, to whom Mr. Whitney's invention had brought in six months more than he had gained from it in fourteen years, said that if that was done Mr. Whitney would become too rich. And the attempt failed.

CHAPTER X

MAKING ARMS

Several years before the term of Mr. Whitney's patent was ended he had come to the conclusion that he would never obtain a fortune from his cotton gin. He therefore made up his mind to go into another business.

His patent affairs had taken him often to the national capital. He was well acquainted there. The president and many of the leading statesmen were his friends. They looked upon him as a man who united remarkable originality of thought with unusual aptitude for work.

When he said that the United States ought to manufacture its own firearms, and that he was thinking of starting a factory for that purpose, he met with encouragement from these men. He was promised orders, and money was advanced by the government to help him establish his factory.

He chose the location of his armory with good judgment. About two miles from New Haven is a rugged mountain, called East Rock. At its foot flows a clear stream whose course is broken by a fall. In this picturesque valley Mr. Whitney built his armory and

ARMORY AT NEW HAVEN

planned to build a mansion. The spot was as convenient as it was beautiful. The waterfall furnished power to run the machinery, and the mountain furnished stone for the walls of the buildings.

The armory was one of the largest manufacturing establishments in the country. All strangers who visited New Haven went to Whitneyville to see it. An observant visitor might read in every detail of the institution, down to the very door fastenings, the boyhood motto of its founder, "Whatever is worth doing at all is worth doing well."

The artistically grouped stone buildings with their arches and gables, the great iron millwheels, the stream walled with stone, and the pretty bridge attracted even the careless visitors.

As the manufacture of arms on a large scale was new work in the United States, Mr. Whitney had to make much of his own machinery and train his workmen. It required skilled artisans to make arms as well as they were made in England, but Mr. Whitney adopted a new plan. Instead of having one man make all the barrels, another all the locks, and so on, he had all the barrels made at one time, all the locks made at another time, and so on. Every man had some one simple thing to do by hand or by machine on each part. This made it very easy for men to learn the trade.

The machinery for the work was so exact that there was no trouble about the parts of the muskets fitting as some had said there would be. Each lock would exactly fit any one of a thousand guns. At first the makers of arms in other countries laughed and said that such a method could never succeed. But they soon stopped laughing, and before long adopted the Whitney method themselves. It is the method used to-day, not only in making arms but in manufacturing almost all complicated articles.

Mr. Whitney's inventions for making arms are said to have shown as much mechanical genius as the cotton gin. But he had had enough to do with patents, and so he got none of those machines patented.

He was kept busy with large orders from the

national and state governments. He found that making instruments of war was much more profitable than his contribution to the arts of peace had been.

The future began to look brighter. The settlement of the cotton-gin struggle relieved him of a great care and much anxiety. The success of his large armory promised independence and comfort for the future.

CHAPTER XI

LAST YEARS

This great inventor, who knew so much about the strong and useful, cared for the gentle and beautiful as well. He had not worked so many years merely that he might be rich in gold and bonds.

He liked beautiful things; he loved refined and educated people; he longed for a happy home. It was to enjoy these blessings that he wished to succeed in business.

He was faithful and tender-hearted. Family and kindred were always dear to him. His sister had been his comrade and confidant. He associated his brother with him in business. Even where he felt no special affection he was always courteous. In his long letters to his father he never forgot to send his best regards to his stepmother.

During the busiest periods of his life he found time to win new friends and enjoy old ones. Men whom he met in business were sure to invite him to their homes, and the ladies he met there always asked him to come again.

He was a tall fine-looking man. The most noticeable features of his strong, kind face were the keen but pleasant eyes and the firm chin. His hair curled slightly over a high forehead.

Though usually dignified and somewhat stately, he could unbend and enjoy a merry frolic with the little folks of his acquaintance, with whom he was a great favorite.

His voice was full and deep, and his conversation was entertaining as well as instructive. Moments snatched from business and spent in pleasant talk were very precious to him.

It is not surprising, then, that as business cares became fewer, he spent much of his time in the society of friends. His carriage was seen frequently in front of Judge Edward's door, and in January, 1817, the distinguished Mr. Whitney's marriage with the judge's youngest daughter was celebrated.

The years that followed were full of happiness. Mr. Whitney was not so wealthy as he deserved to be, but he could completely forget past disappointments and wrongs in the pleasures which he derived from his home and friends.

He enjoyed inventing little things for the house. Once he made Mrs. Whitney a fine bureau. It was fitted with many drawers that were all locked by locking the top one. It was easy to keep mischievous children and prying servants out of that bureau. Mrs. Whitney thought it a wonder and her husband the cleverest man in the world. And the inventor thought his wife's pleased surprise and her bright smiles the best reward in the world.

Surely no other children ever had so many ingenious toys as Mr. Whitney contrived for his happy little ones, and I am sure he got as much pleasure out of them as they did.

We are glad to know that the closing years of his life were happy and peaceful.

He died in 1825, and was buried in the New Haven cemetery. A costly monument marks his grave. A beautiful street in New Haven bears his name. But his invention of the cotton gin is his greatest monument.

THE STORY OF
SAMUEL F. B. MORSE

SAMUEL F. B. MORSE

CHAPTER I

THE PARSONAGE

Long ago in the days when George Washington was president of the United States, a comfortable dwelling stood at the foot of Breed's Hill on the main street of Charlestown, Massachusetts. There was a big knocker on the front door of this house. That was not strange, for many front doors in Charlestown had large brass knockers, and this was no larger and no handsomer than others. But probably no other knocker in the quiet little village was used so often in the course of a day as this particular one.

Men in broadcloth and men in homespun used that knocker. Liveried coachmen with powdered wigs gave dignified raps therewith, to announce the arrival of dainty ladies clad in rustling silks. Women in tidy calico gowns tapped gentle, neighborly taps with it. Important-looking men, on horseback, muffled in long black traveling cloaks, sometimes hammered away with respectful moderation. Poor people with sad faces and shabby garments came too, with modest, timid taps.

The door opened wide to all. Some stayed within only a few moments; many made longer visits. But nearly all left looking well pleased with the world. For this was the home of Mr. and Mrs. Morse, and no one could look cross or unhappy after a visit with them.

Mr. Morse was a Congregational clergyman. He was a good preacher, and often his sermons were printed. He once sent to George Washington, with whom he was acquainted, a sermon on the duties of citizens of the United States, and the president wrote him a pleasant letter to thank him for it.

The First Congregational Church was filled every Sunday with men and women who were eager to hear what Mr. Morse had to say on religious matters. The church members were fond of their able preacher, and when he got married they showed their affections by the presents they gave to help furnish his house. He sent a list of these gifts to his father and here it is: "An iron bake-pan and teakettle; a japanned box for sugar; three iron pots, two iron skillets, a spider, loaf of sugar, mahogany tea table, five handsome glass decanters, twelve wine-glasses, two pint-tumblers, a soup-tureen, an elegant tea set of china, two coffee pots, four bowls, a beautiful lantern, a japanned waiter." Some of these seem to us rather odd wedding presents, but Mr. Morse was well pleased with all of them. The simple, inexpensive articles prove that the poor as well as the rich wished to show their good will to their preacher.

Mr. Morse's influence extended beyond his church. He was widely known and respected. He was a graduate of Yale College; and had read and studied more than most men of his time. Distinguished foreigners traveling in America often brought letters of introduction to Mr. Morse and were entertained at his home.

Because he was a wide-awake man, interested in all questions of public importance, his own countrymen and fellow townsmen liked to discuss questions of the day with him. Business men were glad to talk over their affairs with a man who had such sound judgment and gave such sensible advice.

But not all of the guests at the parsonage came to see the tall, dignified young preacher who looked so grave and stern and talked so pleasantly. Mrs. Morse had many friends of her own. She belonged to a distinguished family. Her father was a judge and her grandfather had been president of Princeton College. She was well educated and very clever. Besides, she was gracious and kind-hearted, and knew how to make everyone feel at ease.

At first, the Charlestown ladies were afraid the young wife from New York would be a little stiff and formal. They were delighted to find her simple and friendly instead. She quite won the hearts of the plainer women by remarking that she liked Charlestown because the ladies were so informal and went calling in calico dresses. This remark was repeated on all sides, and the ladies soon felt free to "drop in" for neighborly visits. Sometimes she spent the afternoon reading to her friends from her favorite books. At other times she sewed, while she chatted with genuine interest about bed quilts, preserves, and other household matters; for she was a fine housekeeper.

When Mr. Morse had distinguished guests Mrs. Morse always helped him entertain them. The "elegant tea set of china" was then brought into use, and the guests were served by their hostess with fragrant tea and golden sponge cake of her own making. All were delighted by her ready wit and lively conversation. Colonel Baldwin, who came often to talk with Mr. Morse about a great canal which was being built under his directions, said afterwards: "Madam's conversation and cup of tea removed mountains in the way of making the canal." Most people found the parsonage an attractive place to spend an evening and soon became deeply attached to Mr. and Mrs. Morse. As time passed they gained a wide circle of friends.

On the twenty-seventh of April, 1791, their first son, the hero of our story, was born, and everyone had high hopes for the child of two such worthy parents. Dr. Witherspoon, the great scholar who had followed Mrs. Morse's grandfather as president of Princeton College, took the little one in his arms and bending his white head over the child, blessed him and prayed that he would live to be as good and great a man as his great-grandfather.

Others were as much interested but not so serious. Dr. Belknap of Boston wrote to Postmaster-General Hazard, in New York: "Congratulate the Monmouth Judge [that was the baby's grandfather] on the birth of a grandson. Next Sunday he is to be loaded with names, not quite so many as the Spanish ambassador who signed the treaty of peace of 1783, but only four! As to the child, I saw him asleep, so can say nothing of his eye, or his genius peeping through it. He may have the sagacity of a Jewish rabbi, or the profundity of a Calvin, or the sublimity of a Homer, for aught I know. But time will bring forth all things."

The four names that the wee, little baby was to be loaded with, were the names of his father, his grandfather, and his great-grandfather—Samuel Finley Breese Morse. They were well known and honored names when they were given to the baby; but they are better known to-day and more highly honored because he bore them.

CHAPTER II

EARLY INFLUENCES

The baby was christened Samuel Finley Breese Morse; and that name was written in the family Bible. But it was too long for every-day use and the child was called simply "Finley" by his parents and playmates.

Little Finley spent the first seven years of his happy childhood in the pleasant parsonage in Charlestown. He was trustful, and quick to make friends, and grew up to be a gentle, affectionate boy, obedient to his parents, kind to his little brothers, and polite to strangers. But he was by no means perfect, and his love of fun sometimes got him into trouble.

His education was begun very early. He was not sent to kindergarten, for there was no kindergarten then. But when he was four years old his father put him in charge of a poor old lady who kept a little primary school. This school was so near the parsonage that Mrs. Morse could stand at the front gate and watch the little fellow until he was safe inside the schoolhouse door. The teacher was known among the village people as "Old Ma'am Rand." That title does not sound very dignified, but the people who used it meant no disrespect to the aged lady. She, poor woman, was so lame that she could not leave her chair.

Now Dame Rand always remembered that the children were sent to her to learn to say their a, b, c's, to count, to spell, to read, and to write. The wee tots did not always remember this, but sometimes seemed to think they were sent to school to whisper and play. At such times the teacher found that she could bring her wayward pupils to order most quickly by using a long rattan rod that reached clear across the room.

One day Finley Morse was so quiet that she forgot he was in the room until she heard the boy who sat next to him laugh. Then she saw that Finley was drawing something on an old chest of drawers which stood at the back of the room. She reached out her long rattan and touched his shoulder. "What are you doing, Finley Morse?" she demanded, so sharply that Finley jumped and looked frightened.

"Just making a picture," he said, hanging his head while his comrade giggled.

"What are you making it with?" she asked.

"This pin," he answered, holding up a strong brass pin.

Then the teacher noticed that the other boy was looking at the drawing as if it were interesting, and she inquired grimly, "What is the picture?"

"A picture of a lady," replied the small culprit, looking exceedingly uncomfortable.

That was enough; the old lady knew quite well

whose picture these little artists liked to draw, and she was not at all flattered by their choice. "Bring the pin to me," she commanded sternly.

The youngster, all unconscious of what was in store for him, meekly obeyed. When he came within reach of the schoolmistress she grasped him firmly and taking the pin, pinned him to her own dress. She looked so severe that Finley was frightened. He screamed and struggled until he tore the teacher's dress and got away.

When Finley Morse was seven years old he had learned all that was taught at Dame Rand's school. His father wished him to have a good education. As there were no good public schools, Mr. Morse decided to send Finley to Andover, first to a grammar school, and then to Phillips Academy, where he should stay until he knew enough to enter Yale College.

Accordingly, as soon as Finley had finished the primary school his little trunk was neatly packed with new clothes, and the seven-year-old boy said good-by to his parents and younger brothers and the dear old home, and went off to live among strangers. He was a manly little fellow and had been brought up to look forward with pleasure to the time when he should be old enough to go away to school. He studied hard and was happy enough at school, but you may be sure he counted the days as vacation approached when he was to go home for a visit.

He was required to write often to his father to give an account of his life at school. His father was such a busy man that the great Daniel Webster said of him, he was "always thinking, always writing, always talking, always acting." Yet he found time to write to his son long letters full of good advice. Finley read these letters over and over again and then put them carefully away. He saved some of them to the end of his life. Here is part of a letter which Mr. Morse wrote to his nine-year-old son:

Charlestown, February, 21, 1801

"My dear Son: You do not write to me as often as you ought. In your next, you must assign some reason for this neglect. Possibly I have not received all of your letters. Nothing will improve you so much in epistolary writing as practice. Take great pains with your letters. Avoid vulgar phrases. Study to have your ideas pertinent and correct, and clothe them in easy and grammatical dress. Pay attention to your spelling, pointing, the use of capitals, to your handwriting. After a little practice these things will become natural, and you will thus acquire a habit of writing correctly and well. General Washington was a remarkable instance of what I have now recommended to you. His letters are a perfect model for epistolary writers. They are written with great uniformity in respect to the handwriting and disposition of the several parts of the letter. I will show you some of his letters when I have the pleasure of seeing you next vacation, and when I shall expect to find you much improved.

Your natural disposition, my dear son, renders it proper for me earnestly to recommend to you to attend to one thing at a time; it is impossible that you can do two things well at the same time, and I would therefore never have you attempt it. . . . This steady and undissipated attention to one object is a sure mark of a superior genius; as hurry, bustle, and agitation, are the never-failing symptoms of a weak and frivolous mind. I expect you will read this letter over several times, that you may retain its contents in your memory. Give me your opinion on the advice I have given you. If you improve this well, I shall be encouraged to give you more, as you may need it."

This letter shows us how much the father expected of his son and how anxious he was to have him improve in every way.

Finley did his best to fulfill his father's hopes. He read and wrote more than most of his classmates. He was especially fond of reading the lives of great men. When he was thirteen years old he wrote an essay on Demosthenes, which was so good that a copy of it was sent to his father who kept it as long as he lived.

When Finley Morse was fourteen years old he finished the course at the academy and was admitted to the freshman class at Yale college. Dr. Morse thought it wise, however, not to send him to college until he was a year older, and so the boy studied at home until the year 1807.

CHAPTER III

COLLEGE LIFE

Dr. Timothy Dwight, the president of Yale College, and Dr. Morse were close friends. When Finley entered college his father wrote to President Dwight asking him to give some attention to the youth, who in spite of his long limbs seemed still a little boy to the affectionate father.

Yale was not so large then as it is now, and the president had an opportunity to get acquainted with many of the students. He took particular pains to be kind to his friend's son. But there never was a boy who stood less in need of a letter of recommendation.

Finley Morse was a fine looking lad, with his father's dignity and his mother's graciousness. Strangers were pretty sure to notice and like him. His teachers were fond of him because he was courteous and studious. He was very popular also with his classmates and took an active part in college life.

The long letters which he sent home regularly were full of news and enthusiasm. Whenever he learned anything that seemed new or wonderful to him, when he got acquainted with an interesting stranger, when he had taken part in any college affair, he thought his father and mother would like to hear about it.

In one letter which is still preserved he told about a meteoric stone which had fallen in Connecticut, not far from New Haven. In another, he told about the trials of the cooks who prepared the food at the college-boys' dining hall:

"We had a new affair here a few days ago. The college cooks were arraigned before the tribunal of the students, consisting of a committee of four from each class in college; I was chosen as one of the committee from the sophomore class. We sent for two of the worst cooks and were all Saturday afternoon in trying them; found them guilty of several charges, such as being insolent to the students, not exerting themselves to cook clean for us, in concealing pies which belonged to the students, having suppers at midnight, and inviting all their neighbors and friends to sup with them at the expense of the students, and this not once in a while, but almost every night. . . . I know not how this affair will end, but I expect in the expulsion of some, if not all, of the cooks."

Although Finley Morse was a leader in students' enterprises he never neglected his work. He did well in all classes, but he was especially interested and successful in chemistry and natural philosophy which were taught by Professor Silliman and Professor Day. It was in Professor Day's natural philosophy class that Finley Morse first became acquainted with the properties of electricity.

One day after a lecture on the mysteries of electricity Professor Day announced that he would try a few simple experiments. He told all the members of the class to join hands; then one student touched the pole of an electric battery and at the same instant every boy in the line felt a slight shock, which, young Morse described as like a slight blow across the shoulders. This experiment was made to give the students some little notion of the marvelous speed with which electricity travels. Next the old laboratory was darkened and a current of electricity was passed through a chain and through a row of metal blocks placed at short distances from one another. The wondering boys saw the flash of white light between the links of the chain and between the blocks.

These simple experiments impressed at least one member of the class so deeply that he never forgot them. Finley Morse said to himself, "Here is a force which travels any distance almost instantaneously, and its presence may be shown at any point in its course by a break in the circuit. This could surely be put to some use in this great world." He wrote to his father giving him an account of the experiments; and, as he could not afford to go home the following vacation, he spent a large part of it making experiments in the laboratory. He had an inquiring mind, and liked to put in practice the theories which he learned in the class room.

During Finley's senior year his two brothers were also at college. One was in the first year, the other in the second. The three young men had great times together. One day they attracted a crowd, by sending up a big balloon from the college campus. This balloon was eighteen feet long. The boys had made it themselves by pasting together sheets of letter paper.

Finley was skillful with his fingers and spent much of his time drawing faces and heads. The walls of his room were covered with crude portraits of his friends.

As years went by he enjoyed this pastime more and more, and though he had had no instruction in drawing and painting, he gradually gained through practice the power of making almost life-like resemblances.

YOUNG FINLEY MORSE'S PICTURE
OF THE FAMILY AT HOME

The first group that he painted is poorly drawn but it is interesting because of the subject. It represents what was probably a typical scene in the Morse household on vacation evenings when the boys were at home. Dr. Morse is standing back of a table with a globe before him. He is evidently explaining something to the members of his family who are grouped around the table in attitudes of close attention. The mother, who sits at one end of the, table, has stopped sewing. The largest boy, who must be the young artist himself, has one hand on her chair, and is leaning eagerly forward. The two younger boys, Richard and Sidney, stand at their father's left. The boys look very quaint and grown-up in their cutaway coats and high stocks. Dr. Morse was the author of a school geography which many of our grandfathers and grandmothers used in their school-days, and he took pains to interest and instruct his boys about far away countries and peoples. This picture was considered by the family a very fine piece of work.

Most of Finley Morse's early attempts at painting were limited to single portraits. As there were no photographers in those days and people liked to have their own and their friends' pictures taken, just as well as we do now, there was a great demand for small portraits or miniatures. Young Morse became so skillful in this work that in his senior year he was able to pay part of his college expenses with the money he earned by painting miniatures. He charged only five dollars for painting a miniature on ivory, and his friends kept him busy with orders.

In 1810, when nineteen years of age, Finley Morse completed his college course, and the grave question of what he should choose for his life work had to be settled.

CHAPTER IV

LIFE IN LONDON

Finley Morse wished to be an artist. He spent the first year after finishing college at his father's home in Charlestown, studying and painting. Dr. Morse was disappointed over his son's decision, but when he found how determined the young man was to be a painter he did all he could to encourage and help him. He wished him to have every opportunity to make a success of the art he loved. He, therefore, agreed to furnish the money needed for three years of study in London, since there were no good art schools in America.

One of the most eminent American painters, Mr. Washington Allston, was then spending a year in Boston. Finley Morse made his acquaintance and arranged to go to London with him the next year, as his student. Accordingly, on the thirteenth of July, 1811, they set sail from New York harbor for England.

It was more than a month after his departure from America before young Mr. Morse sat down in his lodgings in London to write the news of his safe arrival to his father and mother. In this letter he said:

"I only wish you had this letter now to relieve your

minds from anxiety, for while I am writing I can imagine mother wishing that she could hear of my arrival and thinking of thousands of accidents which may have befallen me. I wish that in an instant I could communicate the information; but three thousand miles are not passed over in an instant, and we must wait four long weeks before we can hear from each other."

He little thought then that the time was coming when news could be flashed across the ocean in a few seconds by means of his own invention.

Although so far from home Mr. Morse was very happy in London. He was so glad to be where he could learn to paint that he cared for little else. He breakfasted every morning at seven, and began drawing at half-past seven. He kept at his work from half-past seven in the morning until five in the afternoon. Then he dressed for dinner; and after dinner he took a little walk or went to visit Mr. and Mrs. Allston who lived near by and were always glad to see him. He was so fearful of wasting a minute that he did not even go around to see the famous sights of the great city. His father had given him some letters of introduction to his English friends. These men would have done what they could to make Dr. Morse's son have a pleasant time while in London if they had known he was there, but the young artist felt that he had no leisure for society, and did not deliver the letters.

There was, however, one man in London whom he was impatient to meet, and a few days after their arrival Mr. Allston took him to visit that man. This person was no other than Benjamin West, the great American artist who had been most highly honored in England. The king himself praised his pictures and had his portrait painted by him. West was president of the Royal Academy. Although he had lived many years abroad he loved his native country and was always kind to American artists.

When Mr. Allston introduced Finley Morse to him he received him kindly for the sake of his country and for the sake of Mr. Allston. But when the old artist who had listened to the praise of kings and princes saw this twenty-year-old American youth stand before his great pictures with his sensitive face aglow with appreciation and admiration, he said to himself, "The boy loves it." And from that moment he felt an affection for Mr. Morse for his own sake. He showed him his pictures and invited him to come to him at any time for help.

Mr. Morse wished to be admitted to the Royal Academy. But before this was possible he must prove himself qualified by making a fine drawing. The first weeks of his stay in London were devoted to that drawing. When it was finished he felt quite proud of it and showed it to Mr. West. The great master was highly pleased.

"It is a remarkable production, and you undoubtedly have talent, sir," he said. "It will do you credit when it is finished."

"Finished," echoed Morse in dismay. "It is finished."

"By no means. See this, and this, and this," said

the older man pointing quickly here and there to imperfections which Mr. Morse recognized as soon as his attention was called to them.

He took the drawing home, and as he examined it with more critical eyes, discovered many places which needed touching up. After another week's work he again visited the artist. "I have finished it," he announced triumphantly.

"Not quite, my friend. Look at this muscle and these finger joints."

The crestfallen artist went to work once more. When he next took it to Mr. West he was greeted with the monotonous, "Very good—go finish it." His patience was exhausted and he said in discouragement, "I have done my best, I can do no more."

"Very well," said Mr. West. "That is all I want. It is a splendid drawing. I might have accepted it as you presented it at first, but that was not your best work. You have learned more by finishing this one picture than you would have learned by drawing a dozen incomplete ones. Success lies not in the number of drawings but in the character of one. Finish one picture, and you are a painter."

This lesson made Finley Morse think of the advice his father had given him when he was a little schoolboy.

After Mr. Morse had got well started in his work he gave a little more attention to the life around him. His father, finding that Finley would not hunt up his friends, wrote to them himself giving them his son's address. They sought him out, and thus the young man met many influential people whose friendship he prized through life. He visited the picture galleries, attended the theater occasionally, and went about the city a good deal. He became acquainted with Charles Leslie, a young American, who, like him, had come to London to learn to paint. These two young men formed a strong friendship.

Mr. Allston and Mr. West thought better and better of the young man the more they saw of him. But they did not neglect to do their duty as his teachers and tell him when he made mistakes. This was difficult for Mr. Allston, as he had a gentle, affectionate disposition, and it hurt him to see his young friend unhappy or disappointed. But he was too true an artist to tolerate poor work.

One afternoon he entered Morse's studio just as the latter was finishing what he believed to be a good day's work. The student looked up from his work with a bright face. He expected to see a look of approval on his teacher's face and to hear an enthusiastic "Excellent." Instead, Mr. Allston stood looking at the picture for some minutes in silence. Then he shook his head and said, "Very bad, sir, very bad." Mr. Morse turned red with mortification. He felt vexed with his friend, but controlled his temper and said nothing. The other went on, pointing to the figure on the canvas, "That is not flesh; it is mud, sir; it is painted with brick dust and clay." As Morse stood off and looked at the work he felt the truth of this criticism so bitterly that he was ready to dash his palette-knife through the canvas. But Mr.

Allston quietly took his palette, helped himself to some fresh colors, and with a few touches, gave warmth and brilliancy to the painted flesh. He then stood by and gave directions while the young man tried his hand at it. When he went away, Finley Morse felt the deepest gratitude towards the friend who had made him realize how poor his work was, and had shown him that it was possible for him to improve it.

While in London Mr. Morse did two pieces of work which were so excellent that they astonished many of the older artists. One was a great painting of the dying Hercules. This picture was admitted to the exhibition of the Royal Academy at Somerset House. The critics spoke highly of it, and it was named among the twelve best pictures in an exhibition of two thousand. The other piece of work that attracted the attention of lovers of art was a cast of Hercules, which took the gold medal at the Adelphi Society of Arts.

During the last year of his stay abroad Mr. Morse tried to make a little money with his brush, but he could not sell any pictures. Frames, canvas, and colors were expensive, and the money his father had given him was nearly spent. He wrote home:

"I am obliged to screw and pinch myself in a thousand things in which I used to indulge myself at home. I am treated with no dainties, no fruit, no nice dinners (except once in an age, when invited to a party at an American table), no fine tea-parties, as at home. All is changed; I breakfast on simple bread-and-butter and two cups of coffee; I dine on either beef, mutton, or pork, baked with

potatoes, warm perhaps twice a week, all the rest of the week cold. My drink is water, porter being too expensive. At tea, bread-and-butter with two cups of tea. This is my daily round. I have had no new clothes for nearly a year; my best are threadbare, and my shoes are out at the toes; my stockings all want to see my mother, and my hat is growing hoary with age. This is my picture in London. Do you think you would know it?"

In August, 1815, Finley Morse started for America. He was rich in knowledge, and experience, and friends, but he was poor in purse.

CHAPTER V

PAINTING

Samuel F. B. Morse, as he now signed his name, opened a studio in Boston. There he found many to praise his pictures but none to buy them. For a while he spent his idle hours inventing a powerful pump. But he was impatient to begin painting, and as no work came to him, he determined to go in search of some.

He knew that in the small villages an artist with a good reputation might succeed in getting some orders for portraits if he were willing to accept very low pay for his services. His father was well known throughout New England as a preacher and writer, and with the help of his friends the artist easily found employment for his pencil among the country people.

He painted portraits in one town until he had no more orders, then he went on to another. He asked only ten or fifteen dollars apiece for his portraits. But living was cheap, and he worked so rapidly that he was able to save money, notwithstanding these low rates. He had supposed that this would be very distasteful work. But he took great satisfaction in earning his own money, and had many pleasant experiences. Indeed, it was on one of these portrait-painting tours that Mr. Morse met the beautiful Lucretia Walker, whom he afterwards married.

Some rich southern friends urged Mr. Morse to try his fortunes in Charleston, South Carolina. His uncle, Dr. Finley, who lived there, invited him to stay at his home. His first experience there was as discouraging as his winter in Boston had been. People were kind and friendly. They admired his pictures, but no one ordered any. He felt humiliated and made up his mind to go north again. Before going, he asked his uncle to let him paint his portrait as a return for all his kindness. This portrait was such a splendid likeness that nearly every one who saw it thought he would like to have Mr. Morse paint his picture also. Before long he had a list of one hundred and fifty people who had ordered portraits at sixty dollars apiece.

Mr. Morse's reputation as a portrait painter was soon made in Charleston. The citizens honored him with a commission to paint a portrait of President Monroe. Mr. Morse had a pleasant stay in Washington and painted a strong portrait. The president and his family liked it so much that they requested Mr. Morse to make a copy of it for them.

By dint of hard work Samuel F. B. Morse had succeeeded as a portrait painter, but he was not content to spend his life painting portraits. He wished to stop painting merely for money. He was ambitious to paint beautiful landscapes and great historic pictures. But there was no opportunity to do such work in Charleston, and so he resolved to return to the North.

Before leaving the South, Mr. Morse, with the help of some of the leading men of Charleston, established an Academy of Fine Arts.

In 1820, Dr. Morse gave up his church in Charlestown, Massachusetts, and moved to New Haven. His son visited him there, and renewed his acquaintance with some of the college professors. Professor Silliman lived near to Dr. Morse, and Mr. S. F. B. Morse became deeply interested in the professor's electrical experiments.

In the fall he left his wife at his father's home and went to Washington to paint one of the great pictures he had planned. The subject of this picture was the House of Representatives. He worked on it fourteen hours a day and had high hopes for it. But although it was considered a splendid picture, he did not make any money from it. He was therefore obliged to resort to portrait painting again.

He tried at Albany, the capital of New York, but got no orders there. Then he determined to seek his fortune in the great, rich city of New York. He knew he would have a hard struggle; but it proved even harder than he had expected. He had no money; he could get no work; his rent and board had to be paid. The only thing to do was to fall back once more on the portrait-painting tours.

After a profitable trip through several New England states, and a pleasant visit with his family, he went back to New York with new courage. This time he succeeded better. He had a few pupils and sold some pictures. In the middle of the year an unlooked-for piece of prosperity befell him. General Lafayette was visiting America. New York city wanted a life-sized portrait of the hero. Mr. Morse was chosen to paint it.

Mr. Morse wrote to his wife at once to tell her about his good fortune. He said: "The terms are not definitely settled. I shall have at least seven hundred dollars, probably one thousand." This seemed quite a fortune to the poor artist. He regretted that instead of going to New Haven for a visit with his wife, he would be obliged by his work to go to Washington. But he wrote home cheerfully: "Recollect the old lady's saying, often quoted by mother, 'There is never a convenience but there ain't one' . . . . I look forward to the spring of the year with delightful prospects of seeing my dear family permanently settled with me in our own hired house in New York."

A month later, on the eighth of February, he wrote Mrs. Morse a glowing account of his arrival at Washington and his meeting with General Lafayette. On that same day his father wrote to him from New Haven a letter full of sorrow telling him that, after a slight illness of two or three days, his fair young wife had died suddenly of heart trouble, and he would never see his beloved Lucretia again.

News traveled slowly by stage coach in those days, and this letter did not reach Mr. Morse until after his wife's funeral. He was almost crushed with grief. His return to New Haven could do no good; but he could not paint, and he wished to be among those who had known and loved his wife. He arranged to meet General Lafayette later in New York, and started immediately for New Haven. After a sorrowful visit there he returned to New York where he finished the portrait of Lafayette, which he afterwards described as follows: It is a full-length, standing figure, the size of life. He is represented as standing at the top of a flight of steps, which he has just ascended upon a terrace, the figure coming against a glowing sunset sky, indicative of the glory of his own evening of life. Upon his right, if I remember, are three pedestals, one of which is vacant, as if waiting for his bust, while the two others are surmounted by the busts of Washington and Franklin—the two associated eminent historical characters of his own time. In a vase on the other side, is a flower—the *heliotrope*—with its face toward the sun, in allusion to the characteristic, stern, uncompromising consistency of Lafayette—a trait of character which I then considered and still consider the great prominent trait of that distinguished man."

The artist's struggle seemed over. Now that he cared less to succeed he received more orders than he could fill. Mr. Morse took an active part in the art life of New York. He organized the National Academy of the Arts of Design, and was made its president.

CHAPTER VI

ABROAD AGAIN

When Dr. Morse died in 1826 he had the satisfaction of knowing that the son, for whom he had made many sacrifices, was regarded as one of the leading artists of America.

Mr. Morse had done much to arouse an interest in painting in America. He had lectured and written on the subject; he had organized the Academy of Fine Arts in South Carolina, and the National Academy in New York; and above all he had used his brush constantly.

He stood at the head of his profession in New York. Rich men who had picture galleries began to think that their collections were incomplete unless they included one or two of S. F. B. Morse's paintings.

The artist realized that his countrymen had the greatest confidence in his knowledge and ability. He wished to deserve their good opinion and thought that it was his duty to go to Italy, the land of artists, to learn what he could from the pictures of the old masters.

When it was known that Mr. Morse was going to Italy to study and paint, his friends and admirers came to him asking him to paint something for them while he was away. One wanted him to copy some heads from Titian for not more than one hundred dollars; another was willing to give five hundred dollars for a little copy of "Miracolo del Servo;" others gave him money, leaving him free to paint what he chose for them. When he was ready to sail he had almost three thousand dollars' worth of orders.

Mr. Morse stayed abroad three years. These were years full of pleasant experiences and successful work. He revisited London and saw his old friend, Leslie, now an eminent artist. Together they talked about their days of study under Allston and West, and laughed over their early struggles and ambitions.

Leslie introduced his American friend to the most prominent English artists. They were all very cordial to the distinguished representative of American artists.

While in Paris Mr. Morse ventured to call on General Lafayette. The general remembered instantly the man who had painted his portrait, and made him most welcome. "I saw in the American papers that you had sailed for Europe, and I expected you to make me a visit," he said. Although then an old man he had not lost his interest in America and was glad to talk about our country's present, past, and future with one of her most patriotic citizens. The two men became good friends. They walked and rode together often, and General Lafayette invited Mr. Morse to visit him at his country home.

Mr. Morse came to know other distinguished men

during his stay in Europe. He and the Danish sculptor, Thorwaldsen, became such good friends that he asked Thorwaldsen to sit for his portrait. He sent this portrait to one of the men who had given him one hundred dollars for painting any picture he might think suitable. This same picture was afterward sold for four hundred dollars. The buyer, hearing that Mr. Morse had expressed a wish to have this portrait that he might present it to the King of Denmark, generously returned it to him.

The American novelist, Cooper, and the American sculptor, Greenough, became friends and associates of Mr. Morse during his travels on the continent.

Mr. Morse spent a large part of his time in art galleries, studying the pictures of the great artists who had lived before him. Sometimes he brought his easel and canvas to the gallery and copied their work as closely as he could. In this way he learned a great deal.

He loved to be in the Louvre, the great art gallery of Paris. He wished every American artist might visit it. Then the idea of painting a picture of it occurred to him. It was a great undertaking and he did not wish to stay away from his own country much longer. But he was so eager to paint this picture that he worked on it from morning till night. A great plague, the cholera, broke out in Paris in the spring of 1832. Hundreds died daily, and almost everyone who could get away fled from the city in terror. Morse, however, stayed quietly there, painting every day as usual, and when the date for his return to America came he had his picture so nearly finished that he could complete it in New York.

CHAPTER VII

AN IMPORTANT VOYAGE

When Mr. Morse started for America on the first of October, 1832, he said to himself: "Few American artists have had such splendid opportunities as I have. I must go home and give my countrymen the benefit of what I have learned. I am forty-one years old now. About half of my life, twenty years, I have devoted to art. I have painted many good pictures and gained the respect of artists in my own country and in Europe. I am able to make a comfortable living for my children with my brush. But that is not enough. I must do some grand work that will be remembered when I am dead—something which will show older countries that though America is young she is a great country and can produce great men."

The good ship, which was bearing him nearer and nearer to that country which he loved even better than fair Italy, was called the "Sully." There was a pleasant company of passengers on board. When they met at the dinner table, hungry from the keen sea air, there were lively talks on all sorts of subjects. Mr. Morse often took part in these conversations.

One day some one told about some experiments with electricity which he had read of. Every one was interested. One man remarked, "I have heard it stated that a current of electricity will pass along a very long wire almost instantaneously."

"That is true," said Dr. Jackson of Boston. "It passes over the longest wires that are used in experiments in less than a second of time. Dr. Franklin used wires several miles long and he could detect no difference in time between the touch at one end of the wire and the resulting spark at the other."

"If that is true and the power can be used in any part of an electric circuit," Mr. Morse suggested; "I should think we might send news instantaneously by electricity."

"It has already been used for giving signals, I believe," one of the company remarked.

"But I mean more than that," explained Mr. Morse; "why could we not write instantaneous letters from New York to Charleston with it?"

All laughed at this odd idea. The ladies joined in the conversation and said that Mr. Morse should let them know when his magic letter-writing machine was ready for use. The Southern people began to complain of the inconvenience of corresponding with friends in the North. Letters from the South were a month reaching New York by coach, so that one's dearest friend might die and be buried before one knew anything about it.

Mr. Morse knew the truth of this too well. He

stopped talking with the others, and after dinner went to a lonely part of the deck where he sat quite still, with his notebook in hand, all the afternoon. Other passengers smiled and said, "Do not disturb the artist. He is trying to decide just what shades he can mix together to get the peculiar blue of the sea for some painting."

But he was not thinking of the color of the sea. His mind was busy with the idea that had flashed into it at the dinner table. He remembered the old experiments in the laboratory at Yale; he remembered the conversations he had had with Professor Day and Professor Silliman in later years; he recalled the lectures on electricity which he had heard Professor Dana give at Columbia College. All that he had ever seen, or heard, or thought about electricity came into his mind and made him think that his notion of writing letters at a distance by means of electricity was no wild dream, but a sensible idea. "It only needs the right man to carry it out. Perhaps I am that man," he told himself. He could not sleep that night, his head was so full of his new idea. He rose early in the morning and was again busy with his notebook and pencil. It was not long before he took some of his fellow passengers into his confidence and told them his plan.

"First," he began "it has been proved that electricity travels with almost incalculable speed—with the speed of lightning, in short. We can have as much electricity as we desire with the help of a good battery; and the direction in which it goes can be controlled by us. We can send it where we wish by providing a copper wire to conduct it. Second, electricity has great force."

"I don't doubt that," interposed one of the listeners. "I saw lightning strike a tree once. But how are you going to control that force and make it do what you wish it to?"

"There is a very simple and well-known way of getting a powerful up-and-down motion by means of electricity," Mr. Morse answered. "Bend a bar of soft iron into the shape of a horseshoe and wind a coil of wire around it. When that wire is charged with electricity the iron becomes magnetic. Magnets strong enough to lift great blocks of iron are made in this way. As soon as the electrical current is broken the horseshoe loses its power and the block of iron falls. By simply supplying and breaking the current repeatedly with the help of such a magnet an up-and-down motion can be obtained."

"I have heard all about the horseshoe electromagnet," interrupted one man impatiently. "But I should think it would make a rather clumsy pen. How are you going to use your force to write?"

"I have thought it all out and made drawings of it," replied Mr. Morse. "At one end of the wire will be the battery and the man who sends the message. At the other end will be the pencil for him to write with and the paper for him to write upon. A long ribbon of paper will be attached to two cylinders turned regularly towards each other by clock work, so that the paper will be wound off of one cylinder upon the other. Above this strip of paper will be a bar swinging freely on a central pivot like a balance. This bar will be made to go up or down like a teeter-board, at the will of the man sending the message. There will be a sharp pencil under the end of the bar over the paper. When that end of the bar goes down and right up again the pencil will leave a dot on the paper. If it stays down while the turning cylinders carry the paper along under it, it will make a line. If it stays up while the paper is turned under it, a space will be left. By combining these dots, dashes, and spaces in various ways a telegraphic alphabet can be made."

"Can you show me how the 'teeter-board' could be made to go up and down?" inquired the man who had asked the first question.

"Why yes. There we shall use the magnet," said the inventor. "There will be a small iron plate at each end of the bar. Over the end which carries the pencil there will be a weak permanent magnet, strong enough to draw up that end of the bar when there is nothing pulling against it. At the other end there will be a strong electro-magnet. When the man writing the letter wishes to make a dot he will send a spark of electricity over the wire and it will magnetize the iron so that the power of the weak permanent magnet will be overcome and the end of the bar under the electro-magnet will go up, forcing the pencil end of the bar down upon the paper. If he wishes to make a dash he can keep on the current and the pencil will stay down on the moving paper, but the moment he breaks the current, up the pencil end will go towards the weak permanent magnet and leave a vacant space on the paper."

All agreed that this was a very fine theory, but they thought it could never be put into practice.

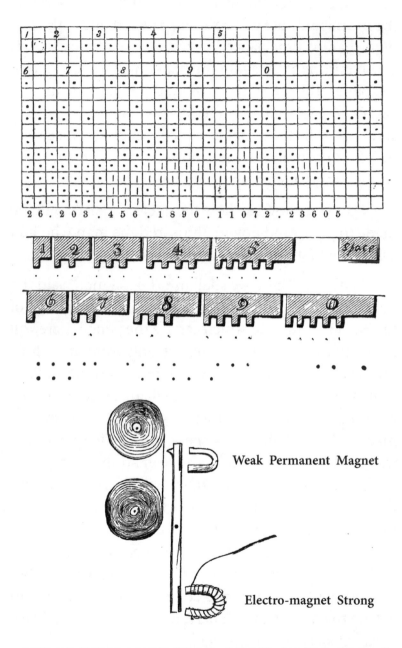

THE DRAWING MADE BY MR. MORSE ON THE "SULLY"

Before the ship entered New York harbor Mr. Morse had filled his notebook with drawings of apparatus for the telegraph. He had also made an alphabet. He had great faith in his plan. One day he said to the captain of the vessel, "Well, Captain, should you hear of the telegraph, one of these days, as the wonder of the world, remember the discovery was made on board the good ship *Sully*." The captain was amused. He regarded the whole matter as merely a visionary dream which even Mr. Morse would soon forget.

CHAPTER VIII

YEARS OF STRUGGLE

When Mr. Morse landed at New York, his two brothers, Richard and Sidney, were at the wharf to meet him. On the way to Richard's house, Mr. Morse told his brothers about his great idea. They were surprised. His last letter had been full of his wishes to paint a great picture. Now he was thinking more about his invention than about pictures. They agreed that it would be a wonderful discovery; and listened to his plan with keen interest. His brother Richard invited him to live at his new home, saying a room had been built and furnished especially for him.

During his first days in New York the artist had many visitors. Friends wished to hear about his trip and to see his pictures. It would have been natural under the circumstances for him to cease thinking about electricity and devote his time to his profession. He was out of money, and many people were ready to buy pictures if he would only paint them. Years of ease, enjoyment, and success lay before him if he chose to give his life to art. Privations, hardships, doubt, must be his portion if he undertook to work out his great invention.

Yet he could not dismiss the telegraph from his mind. The more he thought of it the more firmly he believed that God had made electricity for man's use. And he thought he could do no work in the world more valuable than to make this marvelous force serve man in the telegraph.

He wished to set up the machinery necessary to test his theory. The proper apparatus could not be bought. He had no money to employ craftsmen to make it for him. He therefore undertook to make it himself.

His first workshop was his brother's parlor where he tried to make an instrument for opening and closing the electric current to regulate the dots, dashes, and spaces. Frequent small accidents and the many interruptions which occurred there, made the inventor think it would be wise to move elsewhere. His brothers, who owned and edited a paper, were putting up a business building down town. When this was done Samuel F. B. Morse took a room in the top story of it. There he lived and worked. There his cot-bed stood. There his neglected easel, and paints, and canvas, and models were stored. There his workbench and lathe occupied the place of honor by the window.

He did not go to see his friends. Few of them felt free to seek him out in his attic chamber. His children were with distant relatives. He lived alone. In the evening when it was so dark that he could not be seen he left his room and went to some grocery, where he bought bread, potatoes, eggs, and such food as he could cook for himself. His clothing was poor and shabby. Could he

MR. MORSE MAKING HIS OWN INSTRUMENTS

have gone to work at once with his experiments it would not have been so trying. But he had to spend days and weeks and months contriving tools and implements.

When the committee appointed to choose artists to paint the pictures for the rotunda of the capitol at Washington overlooked Morse and assigned the work to foreign artists, the New York artists were indignant that their leader should be so slighted. They remembered how ready he was to use his influence for their advancement, and how free to share his knowledge with those who needed instruction.

They wished to show their appreciation of all that he had done. They went to work quietly and secured subscriptions to the amount of three thousand dollars from artists and from others interested in art. This they sent to Mr. Morse with the request that he should paint a great historical picture. They said that when it was finished he might do with it as he pleased. Their only wish was to make it worth while for him to paint such a picture, which they were sure would do credit to America and to all American artists.

When Mr. Morse learned what his fellow artists had done he was deeply moved by their kindness. He exclaimed, "I have never heard or read or known of such an act of professional generosity." He resolved to paint a picture that would prove to them that their confidence in him was not misplaced. But he found that he could not put his heart into the work. He was worried about his invention. It seemed much more important than painting pictures. He finally returned the money with the request that his friends would free him from the engagement.

In 1835 Mr. Morse was made Professor of the Literature of the Arts of Design in the New York City University. He moved from his attic quarters to his rooms in the new university. There he fitted up a very rude electric telegraph. It was made in such a rough fashion that he was almost ashamed to show it to his friends. But, in spite of its crudeness, it actually worked. In that room at the university he sent the first telegraphic messages ever carried by electricity.

Every day he had to leave his absorbing experiments to spend hours teaching young art students to paint. He was glad to have this means of supporting himself, but it interfered greatly with his work.

CHAPTER IX

ENCOURAGEMENT

In 1837 Mr. Morse asked some friends to come into his room to look at his telegraph and see it at work. One of his guests was a student, Mr. Alfred Vail. This young man was deeply impressed with what he saw. He soon afterwards called on Mr. Morse alone to ask some questions.

"Your wire here is not long. What reason have you to believe that your telegraph will act successfully at great distances?" he inquired.

"If I can succeed in working a magnet ten miles away, I can go round the globe," answered the confident inventor. "I have contrived a way of renewing the current with a relay. It would not be worth while to have these relays closer than ten miles from each other. But if I can get a force strong enough to lift a hair at a distance of ten miles I can send a current around the earth. Experiments have been made with wires several miles long, and I have faith that the current can be sent ten miles or further without a relay."

Mr. Vail then asked Mr. Morse why he did not push his experiment more rapidly, and when he learned that the delay was caused by lack of money, he offered to supply the funds needed if Mr. Morse would take him into partnership. Mr. Morse was willing to do so; and the terms of the partnership were soon agreed upon. Mr. Vail's father and brother owned large iron and brass works at Speedwell, New Jersey. His knowledge of iron and brass work was of great service to Mr. Morse in perfecting the mechanical part of his invention.

The partnership was formed in September, 1837. Later in the month Mr. Morse applied to the United States government for a patent on *The American Electro-Magnetic Telegraph.*

Mr. Vail promptly furnished the length of wire needed to make the experiments on the result of which depended the success of the invention. With the help of Professor Gale, of the university, Mr. Morse made those experiments and found that he could manage the magnet through more than twenty miles of wire without a relay.

This was as far as he could hope to carry his investigation without help from the government. To construct and operate a telegraph line on a large scale would be too costly a venture for an individual.

Just at this time the government was making inquiries concerning the various telegraphs which were being invented. Mr. Morse sent the United States Treasurer an account of his recording telegraph and was asked to exhibit his instrument at Washington.

Before taking his telegraph to Washington, Professor Morse invited his New York friends to see his invention in operation. Among his guests on this occasion were many who had regretted that New York's greatest artist had "lost his head over a wild scheme." They were amazed to see the results of what they had considered his "wasted years."

The guests whispered messages to him. The instrument went "click! click!" and dots and dashes began to appear on the strip of paper at the other end of the wire. Then some man who understood the telegraph alphabet read the messages to their surprised senders. The New York newspapers gave full accounts of the affair, and people began to think that after all there might be something in the telegraph.

The most distinguished body of scientific men in America, known as the "Franklin Institute," invited Mr. Morse to visit Philadelphia and exhibit his telegraph before the Committee of Science and Arts. They were so favorably impressed with the invention that they recommended that the government give the inventor means to test it on an extensive scale.

Mr. Morse then went to Washington, where the president, the cabinet officers, and many prominent men saw the telegraph at work, and were filled with astonishment and satisfaction.

Mr. F. O. J. Smith, an influential man, desired to have a share in the invention. Mr. Morse thought favorably of his proposal. A company of four partners was formed. In this company Mr. Morse had nine shares; Mr. Smith, four; Mr. Vail, two; Professor Gale, one. Affairs looked encouraging; it seemed probable that Congress would make an appropriation of thirty thousand dollars to give the telegraph a test on a large scale.

Mr. Morse and Mr. Smith went abroad to see about getting patents in foreign countries. In England the attorney general refused to consider Mr. Morse's application for a patent, because a description of his telegraph had already been published and that, he said, rendered the idea public property.

In France, Mr. Morse was shown the greatest kindness. Such eminent scientists as M. Arago and Baron Humboldt were eager to know the American inventor and to see his telegraph.

The fact that space had been so conquered by man that, with a little machinery, messages might be sent to all parts of the world in an instant, seemed too wonderful to be believed. But although everybody wondered and admired, France was the only European country to grant the inventor a patent.

CHAPTER X

WAITING AT LAST REWARDED

In the year 1840 the United States government issued to Mr. Morse the patent which he had applied for in 1837, before going to Europe.

Mr. Morse returned to America full of enthusiasm. Success seemed close at hand. He found, however, that Congress was interested in other matters. The general opinion seemed to be that it would be extravagant to put so much money into an experiment whose outcome was exceedingly doubtful. Soon, even Mr. Morse's partners lost heart and, gave their attention to affairs which would bring them some immediate return.

Poverty made it impossible for the inventor to push the project further without help. He was so poor that he sometimes had to go hungry. He took up his work at the university once more and taught young men to paint.

There was another way in which he was able to earn a little money. While in France he had met Monsieur Daguerre, who had discovered a way to "paint with sunbeams," or take pictures, which were called in his honor daguerreotypes. Morse learned his methods and was the first to introduce the new art of picture making into America. He gave instruction to many young men who wanted to learn Daguerre's process so that they might go around the country making daguerreotypes.

While obliged to spend some time on tasks by which he could earn a living, Professor Morse never ceased to hope and to work in the interest of the telegraph. He employed an agent at Washington, but finding that he accomplished nothing, determined to go there himself and make one more effort to secure the aid of Congress. His partner, Mr. Vail, who had always been so hopeful and ready to help, now said that he could do nothing more, and Mr. Morse was left to do what he could alone.

At length a bill recommending the appropriation of thirty thousand dollars for testing the Morse telegraph was brought before the House of Representatives. Mr. Morse was very much afraid the bill would not pass the House. He sat in the gallery while it was being discussed. Some of the members ridiculed the bill and made jokes about the telegraph. But when the votes were counted there was a majority of six in favor of the appropriation.

After passing the House of Representatives the bill had to go to the Senate. Mr. Morse knew that many of the senators were in favor of his telegraph and he felt confident of victory there. But as the days went by a new doubt troubled him. It was almost time for the Senate to close, and there was so much business to be considered that there was little prospect of his bill being acted upon. The last day came. There were one hundred and forty bills to be disposed of. All day Mr. Morse sat anxiously in the gallery. His friends warned him to give up hope. Late at night he went to his hotel with a sad heart.

He had given ten years of his life to perfect the most wonderful invention of the age. He had succeeded, but his work had been treated with indifference. He felt almost hopeless. But he was too great a man to yield wholly to disappointment. He made all preparations to leave Washington early the next day. Then he went to bed and slept soundly.

The next morning Mr. Morse was a little late for breakfast. As he entered the dining room a servant told him that a young lady was waiting in the parlor to see him.

He was surprised to find that his morning visitor was Miss Annie G. Ellsworth, the daughter of his particular friend, H. L. Ellsworth, Commissioner of Patents.

Going forward to take the young lady's outstretched hand, he exclaimed, "What brings you to see me so early in the day, my young friend?"

"I have come to congratulate you," she answered, her face bright with smiles.

"Indeed! For what?" he asked perplexed.

"On the passage of your bill."

"No, you are mistaken. The bill was not passed. I was in the senate chamber till after the lamps were lighted and my friends assured me there was no chance for me," he returned, shaking his head soberly.

"No, no!" she insisted earnestly. "It is you who are mistaken. Father was there at the adjournment at midnight and even saw the president sign his name to your bill. This morning he told me I might come to congratulate you."

At first Mr. Morse was so surprised and overcome by this piece of good news that he could scarcely believe it. When he realized that it was true, he said: "You were the first to bring me this welcome news, Annie, and I promise you that you shall send the first message over my telegraph when it is done."

"I shall hold you to your promise," the young girl answered happily.

Disappointment was turned to joy. He hastened to write the good news to his partners and friends. He wished that his telegraph was ready for use so that he might instantly scatter the glad tidings to the world. He did not leave Washington that day.

CHAPTER XI

THE TELEGRAPH

The appropriation made by Congress was large enough to build a telegraph line forty miles long. It was decided that the first line should extend from Baltimore to Washington. The work was begun without delay. Mr. Morse took charge of it himself.

At first the wires were put in tubes and buried in the ground. But that did not work well. Mr. Morse then tried putting them on poles in the open air. This proved a much cheaper, quicker, and more satisfactory method.

On the first of May the National Whig Convention was held in Baltimore, to nominate candidates for the presidency and the vice-presidency. Twenty-two miles of wire were up. Mr. Morse thought it would be interesting to announce convention news in Washington by means of telegraph.

There was a railroad between Baltimore and Washington which ran near the telegraph line. Mr. Morse accordingly arranged to have Mr. Vail get the latest news from the train and telegraph it to him in Washington. This was done and the passengers on the first train to Washington after the nomination of Henry Clay found that the news had reached the capital long before them.

On the twenty-fourth of May, 1844, the telegraph line was finished. Mr. Morse was at Washington; Mr. Vail, at Baltimore. Everything was in good working order. It was announced that the first message was to be sent. Crowds gathered around the office.

Mr. Morse remembered his promise to Miss Ellsworth. He sent to ask her what the first message should be. She wrote the noble line from the Bible, "What hath God wrought!" Mr. Morse was greatly pleased with the selection. He said afterward, "It baptised the American telegraph with the name of its Author." And all agreed that the work seemed greater than man's work.

Mr. Morse sent the message to Mr. Vail. It looked like this:

— —	. . . .	. — —	. —	. . . .	. —	—
(w)	(h)	(a)	(t)	(h)	(a)	(t)

. . . .	— — —.	.	. .	—..	. — —	. . . . .	.. —	— — —
(h)	(g)	(o)	(d)	(w)		(r)	(o) (u)	(g)

. . . .	—
(h)	(t)

When Mr. Vail received the message he sent it back to Mr. Morse to let him know that it had reached him all right. It had flown from Washington to Baltimore and back, eighty miles, in a moment.

After the first message, Mr. Morse and Mr. Vail carried on a lively conversation for the entertainment

ALPHABET.		NUMERALS.	
A	· —	1	· — — ·
B	— · · ·		
C	· · ·	2	· · — · ·
D	— · ·		
E	·	3	· · · — ·
F	· — ·		
G J	— · — ·	4	· · · · —
H	· · · ·		
I Y	· ·	5	— — —
K	— · —		
L	————	6	· · · · ·
M	— —		
N	— ·	7	— · · ·
O	· ·		
P	· · · · ·	8	— · · · ·
Q	· · — ·		
R	· · ·	9	— · · · —
S Z	· · ·		
T	—	0	———
U	· · —		
V	· · · —		
W	· — —		
X	· — · ·		
&	· · · ·		

CHARACTERS USED IN SENDING MESSAGES

of those looking on: "Stop a few minutes," said Mr. Morse. "Yes," Mr. Vail answered. "Have you any news?" "No." "Mr. Seaton's respects to you." "My respects to him." "What is your time?" "Nine o'clock, twenty-eight minutes." "What weather have you?" "Cloudy." "Separate your words more." "Oil your clockwork." "Buchanan stock said to be rising." "I have a great crowd at my window." "Van Buren cannon in front, with a fox-tail on it."

A few days later the Democratic National Convention was held in Baltimore. As soon as the candidates were nominated the announcement was sent to Washington by wire. The man named for the vice-presidency was at Washington and received immediate notice of his nomination. He replied by telegraph that he declined. When his message was read in the convention a few minutes after the nomination was made, it caused a sensation. To some this rapid communication seemed almost like witchcraft. Many refused to believe that the message really came from the nominee. A committee was sent to Washington to see about it. Of course the committee found that the telegraph had told the truth.

During the first year the telegraph was put in the hands of the post office department of the government. A tax of one cent was charged for every four characters. The income at the Washington office for the first nine days was as follows: during the first four days only one cent; on the fifth day, twelve and a half cents; the sixth day was Sunday and the office was closed; on the seventh day, sixty cents; on the eighth day, one dollar and thirty-two cents; on the ninth day, one dollar and four cents.

Mr. Morse was amused to see the astonishment his telegraph aroused. His own faith in its success had been so strong that he was surprised to find that others had doubted. The newspapers were full of praises for the inventor and his invention; the mail brought him letters of congratulation from all over the world; he was invited to dine with the highest officers of his own country and with ambassadors from foreign lands.

Mr. Morse offered to sell his telegraph to the government for one hundred thousand dollars. The government declined his offer. The reason given was that the expense of operating it would be greater than the revenue that could be derived from it.

A private company was formed and other telegraph lines were soon built. In 1846 the line between New York and Washington was finished and "the Hudson and Potomac were connected by links of lightning."

Mr. Morse went to Europe again in 1845 in the hope of securing patents. He was received everywhere with honor, but he failed in the purpose of his voyage.

In 1846 Mr. Morse's patent was reissued in the United States. He was troubled, however, as most inventors are, by men who claimed his idea as their own, and pretended to be the original inventors of the telegraph. He was compelled to protect his rights repeatedly by going to court. The question was finally carried before the Supreme Court of the United States. After a thorough investigation the judges all agreed that Mr. Morse was the original and only inventor of the Electro-Magnetic Recording Telegraph.

For some time short telegraph lines were built and operated by separate companies. In 1851 the Western Union Telegraph Company was formed to build a line from Buffalo to St. Louis. This company gradually bought and built other lines until it controlled all the

important telegraph lines from the Atlantic to the
Pacific and from Canada to the Gulf of Mexico.

CHAPTER XII

THE CABLE

Mr. Morse was often heard to say, "If I can make the telegraph work ten miles, I can make it go around the globe." He had shown that it could be made to work across continents. But there was some question as to whether it could be made to cross seas.

In 1842, on one moonlight night in October, Mr. Morse made an attempt in a small way to prove that it could be done. As water is a good conductor of electricity it could conduct the electricity away from the wire. The wire, therefore, had to be carefully covered so that the water could not reach it. Mr. Morse insulated the wire for his first experiment by wrapping it in hempen strands which were afterwards covered with pitch, tar, and rubber. This cable, two miles in length, was wound on a reel and placed in a rowboat. When night had fallen and all was quiet in New York harbor, a small boat put out from the shore. There were two men in the boat. One rowed while the other sat in the stern and unwound yard after yard of the slender cable. The man at the stern was Mr. Morse. At dawn the next day he was up, trying to send messages over the first submarine telegraph in the world. To his surprise, after transmitting a few words the wire ceased to do its work, and no wonder! a ship in the harbor had caught the cable with her anchor, the sailors had dragged it on deck, and not knowing what it was, cut out a piece of it and sailed away.

Ten years later when an attempt was being made to establish electrical communication between the island of Newfoundland and the American continent, the idea of laying a cable across the Atlantic occurred to Mr. Cyrus W. Field. He consulted Mr. Morse, who encouraged him to undertake the work. Soundings had proved that there was in the ocean bed an almost level plateau between Newfoundland and Ireland. This would form a safe bed for the cable to rest on. A company was formed to construct a trans-Atlantic cable. Mr. Morse was made the electrician of the company.

LONGITUDINAL
SECTION OF CABLE

The first difficulty lay in finding a perfectly waterproof cover for the wire, which would help to form a light and flexible but strong cable. Then came the question of laying the cable without breaking it.

The first attempt was made in 1857. The cable then used was twenty-five hundred miles long. The wire was insulated by gutta percha, and that was protected by a twisted wire rope. "The flexibility of this cable was so great that it could be made as manageable as a small rope, and was capable of being tied round the arm without injury. Its weight was but one thousand and eight hundred pounds to the mile, and its strength such that it would bear in water over six miles of its own length if suspended vertically."

VERTICAL SECTION
OF CABLE

The greatest care was observed in running the cable off of the reel to see that there should be no strain upon it. But, in spite of the strength of the cable and the care and skill of those who laid it, the slender rope snapped and the cable so carefully made lay useless, at the bottom of the sea.

Another company was organized, another cable was made, another expedition was fitted out. Another strand snapped, and another valuable cable was lost.

The third attempt was partly successful. The cable was laid and for a few days gave good service. Then for some unaccountable reason it failed to work. The fourth attempt was a failure, but the fifth, made in 1866, proved, to the satisfaction of all, that Samuel F. B. Morse did not exaggerate when he said it was possible to send an electrical current round the globe.

CHAPTER XIII

THE INVENTOR AT HOME

Mr. Morse was an artist and loved beauty. Through most of his life he had been obliged to deny himself beautiful things. He was a quiet, home-loving man. He had been so poor that he had not even a cottage home of his own.

The first money he made from his telegraph was given to charity. As his fortune increased he decided to satisfy his desire for a beautiful home. He selected a picturesque grove on the Hudson River where he built a fine house which looked like an Italian villa. Because of the great locust trees growing there, he named his home Locust Grove.

At this home Mr. Morse assembled the children (now grown up) from whom he had been so long separated; thither he brought his second wife; there he entertained the friends who had been faithful in the old, toilsome days; there he received distinguished visitors from many lands.

The inventor lived quietly and happily at Locust Grove. Sometimes, when he was an old man with snowy beard, he might be seen enjoying the summer air under

MORSE AND HIS FRIENDS AT LOCUST GROVE

his fragrant trees while his grandchildren played about him in the grass. But he liked best the great library where he had collected the books, the pictures, the statues which he had wanted so long.

The latter part of his life was not, however, spent in seclusion. As his fortune grew, his social and business obligations increased. In the winter time he left Locust Grove and lived in a stately mansion in New York city. He was a man of importance and influence, well known throughout America and Europe.

He died in 1872.

THE STORY OF
THOMAS EDISON

THOMAS A. EDISON

CHAPTER I

EARLY YEARS

Often in America the children of humble parents have become distinguished men. Some have gained respect by their wise management of public affairs; some are honored because they led our armies to victory; and some are admired by reason of the beautiful stories and poems which they have written. A few men have earned the gratitude of the people by adding to the comfort and happiness of every-day life through their wonderful inventions. Of these last, Thomas Alva Edison is one of the best known examples.

This great inventor may well be called a "self-made" man. His parents were humble people with only a few acquaintances and friends. The father was a hardy laboring man, who came from a family that worked hard and lived long. Mr. Edison made shingles with which to roof houses. He made good shingles, too. At that time this work was not done by machinery, but by hand. Mr. Edison employed several workmen to help him. He was industrious and thrifty.

When Thomas Edison was born, on the eleventh of February, eighteen forty-seven, the shingle-maker lived in Milan, a village in Erie county, Ohio. His home was a modest brick cottage on Choate avenue. The house was built on a bluff overlooking the valley where the Huron river flows, with the canal beside it.

BIRTHPLACE OF THOMAS A. EDISON

In harvest time the little village was a busy place. All day huge farm wagons drawn by four or six horses rumbled along the dusty roads, carrying grain to the canal. For the farmers from far and near brought their grain to Milan to send it by canal, to Lake Erie. Often as many as six hundred wagon loads of grain came to the village in a single day. The narrow canal was crowded with barges and sailing vessels which were being loaded with it.

Little Thomas Edison was not content to watch this busy scene from his home on the hill. At a very early age he went with the older boys to have a closer view. He soon learned to go about the village, and, when he was no older than many children who are never allowed outside of the nurse's sight, he trotted about alone and felt very much at his ease among the farmers and rough workmen.

Thomas was a serious looking child. He had a large head covered with a wayward shock of hair, which would not curl nor even part straight. He had a broad, smooth forehead, which was drawn into wrinkles when anything puzzled him. His big eyes looked out from beneath heavy brows, with wonder in childhood, with keenness when he grew older. Whenever his brow scowled, his thin lips were pressed tightly together. Even when the child smiled his chin looked very square and firm. The strangers who noticed him said, not, "What a pretty child," but, "What a smart-looking boy!"

The father believed that the best thing he could do for his son was to train him to be industrious. The mother had been a school teacher. She considered an education an important part of a boy's preparation for life. Both parents began early to do what seemed to them their duty towards their son. His father required him to use his hands. His mother taught him to use his head.

He was an eager pupil. An old man in Milan remembers seeing Edison, when he was a youngster in dresses, sitting upon the ground in front of a store, trying to copy the store sign on a board with a piece of chalk. He went to school very little. He could learn much faster at home, where he did not have to go through the formality of raising his hand every time he wanted to ask a question; he wanted to ask a great many.

When Edison was still a mere child, a railroad was built through Milan. Then the farmers used the railroad instead of the canal for shipping their grain. For that reason there was less business in Milan than before the road was built. Many families that had done work in connection with the canal moved away. The place became so dull that Mr. Edison found it hard to make a living there. Accordingly, when Thomas was seven years old, Mr. Edison moved his family to Port Huron, Michigan.

Mr. Edison once said that his son had had no childhood. We have seen that as a child he was a little "sobersides," too busy getting acquainted with the world around him to care for play. As he grew older, his face lost its solemn look. He became an active fun-loving boy. But he differed from other boys in that he found his "fun" in doing things which most boys would have called work.

CHAPTER II

YOUTHFUL BUSINESS VENTURES

When Thomas, or Alva (he was called by his middle name during his boyhood) was twelve years of age, his father considered him old enough to earn his own living. He was therefore willing to have him take a position as train boy on the Grand Trunk Railroad.

Young Edison was just the person to enjoy a train boy's life. He was fitted to make a success of the business. Forward and self-confident, he had a pleasant, jovial manner which made him popular with strangers. He was quick-witted enough to say just the thing about his wares to amuse or interest the passengers. And he sold enough newspapers and sweetmeats to clear a good profit.

Besides, he was shrewd and self-reliant. Finding that the sale of papers depended on the news they contained, he looked them over carefully before buying, and soon learned to judge accurately the number he could sell.

The Civil War was then going on, and when there was exciting war news, papers were in great demand.

One day he opened the paper and found an account of the battle of Pittsburg Landing. He said to himself, "I could sell a thousand of these papers, if I had them, and if the people at the stations only knew there had been a battle." Here were two big "ifs," but the boy promptly made up his mind how to overcome them.

He went to the telegraph office and sent dispatches to the towns at which his train stopped, announcing that a terrible battle had been fought. He felt sure that the news would spread rapidly through the villages, and crowds would be at the stations waiting for the papers.

He then went to the newspaper office and asked the business manager to sell him one thousand copies of the Detroit Free Press, on credit. The manager refused curtly. Nothing daunted the boy sought the office of the editor, Mr. W. F. Story. "I am the newsboy on the Grand Trunk Railroad, from Detroit to Port Huron, and I should like to have one thousand copies of to-day's 'Press,' containing the account of the battle," he said blandly. "I have no money to pay for them, but I am sure I shall be able to pay you out of the proceeds of the day's sale."

The editor looked at him in surprise. "And where do you expect to find purchasers for so many papers?" he asked. When he heard what the youth had done to secure his customers, he smiled and gave him an order for the papers.

Edison was not mistaken; he found his papers in such demand that he was able to raise the price first to ten cents, then to twenty-five cents. He made what seemed to him a fortune out of the day's work.

Profit in money was not, however, all that Thomas Edison gained from his experience as train boy. The busy, varied life he led was in many ways an education to the active, wide-awake boy. While attending to his work he gave it his undivided attention. But when he had finished it, he dismissed it from his mind and interested himself in other things.

He learned a good deal about the country through which he traveled every day. Most boys are thoroughly well acquainted with the one town in which they live, but he knew Detroit as well as Port Huron, and was familiar with the geography and business of the country and villages between those cities.

His train was a mixed train, made up of freight and passenger cars. The newsboy considered himself a very important part of that train. He knew it from engine to caboose, and was on good terms with all the trainmen. Indeed, he felt an interest and pride not only in "my train," but in "my road," as he called the Grand Trunk Railroad. He knew its officers, its trainmen, its station agents, the telegraph operators, and even the trackmen. He could always be depended upon for the latest railroad news either in the nature of business or personal gossip.

Finding that others were as much interested as he in what was going on along the road, but were slower in finding it out, he decided to print a railroad newspaper. He got some old type from the office of the "Detroit

Free Press" where he had made friends, and set up a printing office in the corner of a freight car. One half of the car was fitted up as a smoker, and the newsboy took possession of the unused half. There, when he had nothing else to do, he worked hard on a paper of which he was proprietor, editor, business manager, reporter, and printer.

He issued his paper weekly and called it "The Grand Trunk Herald." It was a small paper consisting of two sheets printed on one side only. It was poorly printed, and the grammar and punctuation were often faulty, but it contained much that was of interest to those who were connected with the railroad. Besides such business items as changes in time, the connections made with the train by stage coaches, and announcements of articles lost and found, it was filled with current railroad news and observations by the editor, which give us a good idea of the character and habits of the boy. Here are some extracts from the "Herald:"

"Heavy shipments at Baltimore; we were delayed the other day at New Baltimore Station, waiting for a friend, and while waiting took upon ourselves to have a peep at things generally; we saw in the freight house of the G. T. R. 400 barrels of flour and 150 hogs waiting for shipment to Portland."

"John Robinson, baggage master at James Creek Station, fell off the platform yesterday and hurt his leg. The boys are sorry for John."

"No. 3 Burlington engine has gone into the shed for repairs."

"The more to do the more done. We have observed along the line of railway at the different stations where there is only one Porter, such as at Utica, where he is fully engaged from morning until late at night, that he has everything clean and in first-class order, even on the platforms the snow does not lie for a week after it has fallen, but is swept off before it is almost down, at other stations, where there is two Porters, things are *vice-versa*."

"Premiums. We believe that the Grand Trunk Railway give premiums every six months to their engineers who use the least wood and oil running the usual journey. Now we have rode with Mr. E. L. Northrop, one of their engineers, and we do not believe you could fall in with another engineer more careful or attentive to his engine, being the most steady driver that we have ever rode behind [and we consider ourselves some judge having been railway riding for over two years constantly] always kind and obliging and ever at his post. His engine we contend does not cost one fourth for repairs what the other engines do. We would respectfully recommend him to the kindest consideration of the G. T. R. officers."

The good-natured self-importance of the young editor, with his pompous editorial "We," is amusing. But though the reader may smile at the fourteen-year-old boy's recommendation of the experienced engineer to the attention of the railroad officer, he feels that the writer must have been a sensible boy and that he knew what he was talking about. Edison's remarks about the well-kept station house show the boy's appreciation of order and punctual attention to duty. What he has to say is sensible and sincere, and it is not surprising that he found readers.

He had over three hundred subscribers for his paper, at three cents a copy. Of course the readers of the "Herald" were all railroad men.

This little sheet gained some notoriety, however, and was mentioned in a London paper as the only newspaper in the world published on a train.

Edison's success with the "Herald "induced him to undertake to print a paper of more general interest. His second paper was called "Paul Pry." In this paper Edison used great freedom in expressing opinions of men and things. On one occasion a personal paragraph in his paper so angered a reader, that, seeing the editor near the river, he gave him a good ducking. This severe punishment dampened the youthful editor's enthusiasm for journalism, and he gave up the business a short time after the occurrence.

CHAPTER III

STUDY

A boy who writes his ideas for others to read is pretty sure to be interested in reading what others have written. This was the case with Edison. He realized that there was a good deal in books that was worth knowing. He had no one to guide him in selecting his reading, but that did not trouble him. Life seemed long, and books were very little things. There was surely time enough for an industrious person to read them all. He determined to begin with the Free Library of Detroit.

He picked out a shelf of particularly large, wise-looking books and commenced reading. Among these books were: Gibbon's "Decline and Fall of the Roman Empire," Hume's "History of England," Burton's "Anatomy of Melancholy," and Newton's "Principia."

A large part of the contents of these books was too advanced for the understanding of the young reader. Nevertheless he kept cheerfully at the task he had set himself, until he had finished all the books on a shelf fifteen feet long.

He had learned a great many interesting facts from this difficult reading. But perhaps the most valuable lessons the experience taught him were about books. He had discovered for himself that it was both impossible and undesirable to read all books; that some had in them very little that was of value to him, and were not worth the time it took to read them, while others deserved the closest study. In fact he had become something of a critic, and was able to judge for himself whether a book would interest and help him. He did not stop reading when he had finished the shelf, but henceforth he chose his books with more care.

Some of the books that he read troubled him, because he could not wholly understand them, and he was always on the lookout for some one who knew enough to explain the difficulties to him. Other books filled his mind with new ideas and made him think very hard. An old chemistry excited him so much that he could think of nothing but the wonderful statements it contained about even such simple things as air, water, fire. He was curious to experiment with some of the strange elements mentioned in it, such as oxygen, nitrogen, and hydrogen. Thomas Edison was not the boy to sit still and wonder when his curiosity was aroused. He thought it would be a fine thing to have a workroom or laboratory, all fitted out with materials and implements for making chemical experiments, and he determined to have one.

His first step towards the realization of this ambition was to get acquainted with a chemist. The next, was to buy such second-hand apparatus as he could with the money he had saved, and get a few of the cheaper chemicals. These he arranged neatly in the corner of the freight car which was his newspaper office. The little bottles with their glass stopples and mysterious contents were exceedingly precious to him, and lest some one should meddle with them, he pasted poison labels on all of them.

In his rude little laboratory the inventor made his first experiments. He found this a very fascinating pastime. He was willing to work hard, dress poorly, and eat plain food for the sake of his laboratory. Without a teacher, with only a book to instruct him, he experimented until he had learned the properties and powers of many chemical substances.

He had accidents occasionally, for although he was careful, he worked under disadvantages on the jolting train. One day a bottle of phosphorus fell from its shelf and broke. The contents set the floor on fire. The fire was put out before it had done much injury; but the conductor was excited and angry. He said he would have no more of the dangerous stuff on his train. To be very sure that he would not, he threw the remaining bottles out of the car, and hurled after them not only all of the laboratory furnishings, but even the printing press. The owner protested with some spirit against the destruction of his property, whereupon the conductor seized him and pushed him out of the car.

Edison had learned in his rough-and-tumble life not to cry over spilt milk. It was discouraging to see the possessions he had collected with so much pains scattered by the roadside. But as soon as he had his fists unclinched the plucky fellow was ready to forgive the hasty conductor. "The old chap got a bad scare," he said to himself. "After all it's a wonder he didn't throw my traps overboard long ago." And he went to work picking up what was left of his printing shop and laboratory, planning the while where he would re-open his shop. He decided that his father's cellar would be the safest place. Before many days, he had made good his loss by new purchases and had begun work on a larger scale than ever.

CHAPTER IV

A CHANGE OF BUSINESS

Edison took up his train duties promptly, without any evidence of ill-feeling towards the conductor who had treated him so harshly. A few weeks after that unpleasant occurrence, the train stopped one morning at Mount Clemens, to take on some freight cars, which were waiting on the side track.

As usual, the train boy, with his papers under his arm, was peering about the station house to see what was going on. Suddenly, as he looked around the corner, he saw the two-year-old son of the station agent, playing on the track, while the heavy freight car that was being backed down to the train, was almost upon him. Without a second's hesitation, the newsboy threw his papers to the ground and plunged forward to save the child. With one flying leap he seized the boy and cleared the track, falling on the gravel beyond, just out of reach of the wheels of the car. The baggage-master, who saw the act and thought that both boys would be killed, gave a shriek which brought every one around the station to the spot.

When the child's father heard the story, he felt so

grateful to the brave boy that he would have been glad to give him a rich reward. He was a poor man, however, and could not express his thanks in money. But there was one thing he could do, to better the boy's fortune. He was a good telegraph operator; he would teach young Edison telegraphing, and get him a position where he could earn twenty-five dollars a month. Taking the boy's hand, he said, "You have saved Jimmy's life, Al, and I'd like to show you how I feel about it. I haven't anything to give you, but if you'll stop off here two or three nights in the week I'll teach you to telegraph and get you a good job."

Edison's face lighted up with pleasure. "I don't want any pay for pulling Jimmy out from under that freight car," he said loftily. "But I would like mighty well to learn to telegraph. Nothing better! If it suits you we'll begin to-night."

The lessons were commenced at once and Mr. Mackenzie, the agent, found his work as instructor really pleasant at first. His pupil came regularly and made such surprising progress that it was a great satisfaction to teach him. But after a few days the train passed and "Al" did not get off. This happened several days in succession. Mr. Mackenzie felt disappointed. "I declare he's like all the rest of them," he mused. "I thought he had some grit. But I've always noticed that when a boy is so quick and learns so fast, he never keeps at it." He was mistaken, however, that time.

That very evening when the train came in, young Edison swung himself off with a beaming face. He carried a small package neatly tied up, which he was eager to show his friend. It proved to be a tiny telegraph instrument which he had made at a gunsmith's shop in Detroit. It was so small that it could be placed on a small envelope, yet it was perfectly complete, and worked well when tested.

The young student in telegraphy had not lost interest, but he had come to a place where he could get along without a regular teacher. He was used to doing things in his own way and at his own time, and having received a good start from Mr. Mackenzie, was able to go on without much further help from him. He had made friends with many of the telegraph operators along the railroad. He now visited their offices to practice his art. He found them all interested in his progress and ready to give him a word of advice when he needed it. In three months' time he had so thoroughly mastered the business that Mr. Mackenzie said the boy knew enough to teach him.

He was not satisfied with being able to work the instrument, to send and receive messages. His inquiring mind wanted to discover how the instrument worked and why. He immediately began to experiment with electricity in his cellar laboratory.

With the help of a friend he constructed a short telegraph line of his own. At first he tried to obtain a current from a very curious dynamo. He had noticed the sparks that may be produced by stroking a cat. Half in fun, and half in earnest, he got two large black cats and tried with much rubbing to create an electrical current, but was obliged to resort to the ordinary battery.

Edison gave up his position as train boy and spent most of his time at the Western Union Telegraph office in Port Huron. When there was more work to do than usual, or when one of the regular operators was not at his post, Edison was hired to work for a short time. He did good work and was soon given a regular position at a salary of twenty-five dollars a month, with the promise of additional pay for extra work.

CHAPTER V

THE BOY TELEGRAPH OPERATOR

Edison worked faithfully in his new position. He did extra work and did it well. But he waited in vain for the extra pay that had been promised him for taking long reports and working out of hours. When he found that the man who employed him did not keep his word, he gave up his position. Mr. Mackenzie soon got him a situation as night operator at Stratford, in Canada.

So far as ability to send and receive messages went, Edison was perfectly capable of filling the place. But he was by no means the slow, faithful, unquestioning, obedient agent to leave in charge of a telegraph office at night. He was a mere boy, only fifteen years of age, and had had no training in working under orders. He could not obey regulations which seemed to him useless, and he sometimes thought he could improve on the directions given him. There was no danger of his neglecting his duty through idleness, but he might neglect it while working out some pet notion of his own.

The manager of the circuit realized that the night

operators might be tempted to shirk their work, and so he required them to telegraph a signal to him every half hour in order that he might be sure they were awake and at their posts. Edison's signal was six.

This was a wise regulation, but Edison did not appreciate the necessity for it. He found it a great bother to keep his eye on the clock and leave his reading or some experiment that he was working out in the quiet hours of night, to report that stupid "six" every thirty minutes. He wondered if he couldn't make a machine attached to the clock that would save him the trouble. After a good deal of thinking and experimenting, he fitted up an instrument that could telegraph "six" as well as he could.

This was a great relief to him, and he felt free to do what he liked with his time without much fear of discovery. He even left the office and made expeditions about town.

One night while he was away, the manager tried to call him up but could get no response. He thought this odd as Edison was more punctual with his signals than any other operator on the line. He waited, then tried again and again, with no better success, though the signals came with their accustomed regularity. He made an investigation, and the young inventor received a severe reprimand for his clever contrivance.

His next offense came near having serious results. He had orders to deliver messages to trains before reporting them back to the dispatcher. One evening, because it seemed easier to do so, he reversed the order and returned the message before delivering it. Then he heard the engine bell ring for the train to start. He jumped up in a hurry, but when he got to the platform, the train was well in motion. The message was an order for the train to wait at a switch until a special had passed. He ran frantically after the train hoping he might catch it at the freight depot, but he could not overtake it.

He ran swiftly back to telegraph his error to the dispatcher, only to learn that it was too late to warn the other train. Now because of his disobedience two great trains were rushing towards each other on the same track. That was a terrible hour for the poor boy. There were chances that the engineers would see each other's engines in time to prevent a wreck; but there were chances that they would not. It was frightful to think of the misery and loss he might be responsible for.

The watchfulness of the engineers prevented a collision. When the special came thundering up the track safe and sound, Edison knew that the danger was over. His disobedience had brought no harm to others, but he felt sure that he would hear more of it.

Nor was he mistaken. The superintendent called him to his office and frightened him with threats of imprisonment. He left town on the next train without even collecting the money due him for his services.

His experience at Stratford had been unfortunate perhaps, but he was a better operator because of it.

He had not only gained in skill, but had learned the importance of obedience in little things.

He spent a few weeks at home out of work. One day when he was down by the St. Clair river, watching the ice which was breaking and piling up across the stream, word came that the electric cable between Port Huron and Sarnia, the Canadian city on the opposite side of the river, had been broken by the ice jam. There was no bridge; the ferryboat could not run on the ice-blocked river; with the cable broken all communication between the places was stopped.

Edison saw a locomotive standing on a track near by, and a thought struck him. He jumped aboard her and whistled a greeting to Sarnia, making short toots for the dots and long toots for the dashes. He repeated his message several times. At last the trained ear of the old operator in Sarnia recognized the familiar signals of the Morse alphabet, and with the help of an engine whistle, sent a reply across the impassable river.

This little incident was very much talked about. People began to say that Thomas Edison was most ingenious.

Good telegraph operators were hard to get, and Edison was not long without a position.

CHAPTER VI

TELEGRAPHER AND INVENTOR

Edison was not a dreamer. He may have had vague notions of doing something great in the distant future, but they did not interfere with the accomplishment of his practical, definite ideas. Having become a telegraph operator, his modest ambition was to be a good one. More than that, he wanted to be able to receive "press reports." That is, he wanted to be able to work so fast that he could handle the long dispatches sent to the newspapers.

That was not an easy task. Indeed for a while he gave up hope of being able to keep up with the clickings of an expert sender, without the help of some mechanical device. If he could only find a way to make those confusing dots and dashes come more slowly!

His busy brain and nimble fingers working together, soon discovered a way to do this. He contrived a repeating receiver, which recorded the message as rapidly as the best sender could send it, and repeated it as slowly as the poorest receiver could wish.

When this repeater was in working order, Edison secured an engagement to take some press-report work.

201

He told the sender to "rush" him. The man did so, but no matter how rapidly he worked, he did not seem to be able to confuse the marvelous receiver. Edison was meanwhile copying slowly from his faithful repeater. He was able in this way to hand in beautifully written, unscratched, and unblotted sheets of report, which aroused the astonishment and admiration of all who saw them.

Soon, however, a report came in that had to be delivered immediately. Then the inventor was in difficulty, and had to admit that he was not such a fast receiver as he seemed.

To invent the repeater, required a higher order of mind perhaps, than was necessary to receive messages rapidly. But Edison felt no pride in that achievement. His object was to be a rapid receiver and nothing else would satisfy him.

He next made a series of thorough experiments in penmanship, to discover which was the most rapid style of writing. After a long and careful examination he decided on the clear, round, upright characters which he used all the rest of his life. It is interesting to notice that this youth was about thirty years ahead of the writing teachers in adopting the beautiful vertical writing, which is taught in many schools to-day.

Obliged to give up press-report work until he had gained greater skill, Edison devoted his time to practicing as the only means of acquiring the speed he desired. He worked all day and, whenever he could get employment, all night, snatching bits of sleep when he could. His constant diligence soon enabled him to work so fast that he was put at one end of a line worked by a Louisville operator, who was one of the fastest senders in the country. His experience at that wire made him as expert as even he desired to be.

But he was not ready to sit down to rest. As soon as one thing became easy for Edison he always began working on something else.

While at Memphis, he constructed an instrument called an automatic repeater, which made it possible to connect separate telegraph lines in such a way as to transfer messages from one wire to the other without the aid of an operator.

He then began to try to discover how two messages might be sent over the same wire at the same time. He spent a large part of his time reading and experimenting with this end in view.

His fellow operators laughed at him and called him the "luny," because he had so many "queer notions" and did not care for the things they enjoyed. He worked constantly, dressed shabbily, and spent most of his money for scientific books and materials with which to make experiments. His gay comrades liked him in spite of his peculiarities. He was ready with jokes and funny stories, and could be depended on to lend an empty-pocketed friend a dollar in the days of scarcity which usually preceded pay day.

His employers were often impatient with him. They thought it strange that a young man who could telegraph so well, was not content to do it, but must needs neglect his work, while he wasted time and kept the office in confusion with some impossible scheme.

This is the reason that for five years Edison roamed from town to town, through the central states, never having much trouble to get a place because he was such a good operator, and never keeping one long because he could not overcome his impulse to invent.

During those five years he suffered a good many hardships and formed very irregular habits of work, often studying and working all night long. But while many of his comrades fell into evil ways, Edison lived a clean, straight life. This was one reason why he was able to work so hard without injuring his health.

CHAPTER VII

IN BOSTON

Edison had a friend in Boston. This man urged him to come East. He said that he would receive a better salary and have greater opportunities for study and invention. When a vacancy occurred in the Boston office, he recommended Edison for the place. And so it happened that when Edison was twenty-one years old, he was called to the great city of Boston.

Here is the account the inventor himself gives of his first appearance in the Boston telegraph office:

"I had been four days and nights on the road, and, having had very little sleep, did not present a very fresh or stylish appearance, especially as compared to the operators of the East, who were far more dressy than their brethren of the West. The manager asked me when I was ready to go to work. 'Now,' I replied. I was then told to return at 5:50 P. M., and punctually at that hour I entered the main operating rooms, and was introduced to the night manager. My peculiar appearance caused much mirth, and, as I afterwards learnt, the night operators consulted together how they might 'put a job on the jay from the woolly West.' I was given a pen and assigned the New York No. 1 wire.

"After waiting upwards of one hour I was told to come over to a special table, and take a special report for the *Boston Herald*, the conspirators having arranged to have one of the fastest senders in New York to send the dispatch and 'salt' the new man. I sat down unsuspiciously at the table and the New York man started slowly. I had long since perfected myself in a simple and rapid style of handwriting, devoid of flourishes, and susceptible of being increased from forty-five to fifty-four words a minute by gradually reducing the size of the lettering. This was several words faster than any other operator in the United States.

"Soon the New York man increased his speed, to which I easily adapted my pace. This put my rival on his mettle, and he put on his best powers, which, however, were soon reached. At this point I happened to look up, and saw the operators all looking over my shoulder, with their faces shining with fun and excitement. I knew then that they were trying to put a job on me, but kept my own counsel and went on placidly with my work, even sharpening a pencil at intervals, by way of extra aggravation.

"The New York man then commenced to slur over his words, running them together, and sticking the signals; but I had been used to this style of telegraphy in taking reports and was not in the least discomfited. Finally when I thought the fun had gone far enough, and having about completed the special, I quietly opened the key and remarked, 'Say, young man, change off, and send with your other foot.' This broke the New York man all up, and he turned the job over to another man to finish."

Men are usually ready to respect real merit. Edison's fellow-workers, on discovering his ability, gave the new comer a cordial welcome among them, in spite of his careless dress.

But better even than that, Edison found his new employer to be a man of high intelligence. He could talk over his ideas with him without fear of being called a "luny." It was a new pleasure to the young man to find sympathy and appreciation concerning the questions that were of the highest interest to him.

The Boston Public Library furnished him with valuable works which he had not been able to obtain in the West. He met men of scientific learning and came in contact with highly skilled artisans.

Everything in his new life stimulated his ambition and encouraged him to attempt great things. Much of the time he felt as he expressed it one morning to a friend: "I've got so much to do and life is so short, I'm going to hustle."

His regular work occupied the night hours. That left the day free. He spent as few as possible of the precious hours in sleep. Having found that he could not carry on his experiments in the telegraph office here, as he had so often done in the West, he opened a small shop of his own. In that shop he spent a large part of each day. Sometimes he devoted all of his time to working on his own inventions. Again, he took orders and did work for others.

He became known in Boston as an authority on electricity, and was even invited to speak on the subject before a school of young women.

He was especially interested at this time in inventing an electrical instrument for recording votes in a great assembly like the House of Representatives. He made an excellent machine that did its work faultlessly, and had it patented. After all his labor and expense he found that legislative bodies did not care for such an accurate and speedy vote recorder. His invention was useless. This was a bitter disappointment to him and he did not forget the lesson it taught him: never invent anything without first finding out whether it is needed.

Having failed with his vote recorder because of his ignorance of parliamentary customs, he returned to the familiar field of telegraphy and once more tried to solve the problem of sending two messages over a wire at one time. There was no doubt that a contrivance which would make that possible would be in demand.

He progressed so well with his experiments that in 1869 he was ready to make a trial of his invention on a large scale.

At this time his engagement with the Western Union Telegraph Company being completed, he resolved to go to New York.

CHAPTER VIII

RECOGNIZED AS AN ELECTRICIAN

Edison's stay in Boston had been pleasant and profitable in many ways, but he felt more and more that New York, the great center of the American business world, was the city of opportunity.

He arrived there with no work and no money. For although he had been a hard worker while in Boston, he had spent so much on experiments and inventions that he was heavily in debt. He did not feel worried for the future, however. He had the greatest confidence in himself and in electricity. He knew that electricity could be made to do marvelous things and that few men knew so well as he how to make it do them.

Failing to get employment in a telegraph office as he had hoped to do, he wandered about, visiting the various establishments maintained in connection with electrical enterprises, in the hope of finding some work. One day as he approached the office of Laws' Gold Reporting Telegraph Company, he noticed an excited crowd of men and messenger boys around the entrance. Coming nearer, he learned that there was something wrong with the electrical instrument which sent the market reports to the brokers' offices, and that if it was not remedied at once, many business men would lose heavily.

He made his way quietly and quickly into the office where he found Mr. Laws almost distracted with anxiety. The apparatus refused to work, and he was so nervous and excited that he could not find what the trouble was. Edison went up, and introducing himself as an electrician, made a rapid but careful investigation. He had been working on an invention somewhat similar and understood the instrument perfectly. He discovered the difficulty and corrected it while Mr. Laws looked on in admiration. His sure, swift movements showed his familiarity with the complicated and delicate mechanism.

This performance won the respect of Mr. Laws as completely as the rapid telegraphing had secured the esteem of the Boston operators. Mr. Laws not only felt grateful, but he immediately recognized in Edison a man whose services were worth having. This incident led to Edison's obtaining regular employment under Mr. Laws at a salary of three hundred dollars a month.

Having accomplished his boyish ambition to be an expert telegraph operator, Edison, at the age of twenty-two gave up that business and started out in a broader field of work. He began at once to make improvements in the machine used by the company he served. Before long he invented a new and better instrument to take its place.

His next important step was to enter the service of the Gold and Stock Telegraph Company. Edison made numerous inventions in connection with the apparatus used by this company. The company considered them so valuable that it offered to buy them all. When the committee representing the company asked Edison how much he would take for his inventions he replied that he did not know what they were worth. He asked what the company was willing to give him. He had decided to accept if offered five thousand dollars. Imagine his surprise when offered forty thousand dollars.

The young man was not long in deciding how to spend his unexpectedly acquired fortune. With it he equipped a larger and more elaborate shop than he had ever had. He now had room, implements, and assistants for working out the schemes which had been simmering in his head ever since he was a boy.

He accomplished so much that he began to be looked upon as a wonder. The Western Union Telegraph Company and the Gold and Stock Telegraph Company feared that rival companies would obtain the use of his patents. So they paid him a large salary to give them the option on all of his telegraphic inventions. This made it possible for Edison to devote his entire time to the work he loved: to making machines which would do well the work which existing machines did poorly.

CHAPTER IX

INVENTOR AND MANUFACTURER

Edison opened a large laboratory and factory in Newark, New Jersey. There he employed three hundred men to assist him in his experiments and to make the contrivances which he invented.

This was a more serious responsibility than he had yet undertaken. It was one thing to tinker away by himself and work out his ideas with his own skillful hands, and quite another to manage and direct three hundred men.

He was not, however, ignorant of human nature. Even when a newsboy he had been busy getting acquainted with people and learning to influence them so they would do as he wished.

In his factory his manner toward his men was friendly and boyishly unconstrained. There was little formality between employer and employees; his men were not afraid of the "boss." He depended on their interest and good-will, rather than obedience to rigid rules, for the best results. His big factory was managed

PATENT OFFICE AT WASHINGTON

with a surprising lack of regularity. If he was anxious to have a piece of work finished all hands were kept over hours. When things went well and some important undertaking was completed, there was a fragment of a holiday.

It is said that when a man asked Edison to what he owed his success, he replied, "To never looking at the clock." He expected from his men something of the same indifference to time and absorption in work that he had always shown.

On one occasion, when an instrument did not give satisfaction and he could not find what was wrong, he took half a dozen of his most able assistants with him to an upper room, saying, "We will stay there until this thing is straightened out." They worked there sixty hours, and at the end of that time came out of their voluntary prison tired, but satisfied and successful.

If Edison demanded a good deal of his men, he was more severe with himself. Many and many a time, after a day's work, he sat all night in his private office or laboratory studying out some baffling problem.

He was very much beloved by his workmen, and if he came back from a business trip to New York, with his boyish face all aglow with satisfaction, and tossed his silk hat up to the ceiling with a cheer for the invention he had just sold, a wave of good feeling and hilarity spread over the whole establishment.

It was in the first year of his life at Newark that Edison married. After a brief and business-like courtship, he married Miss Mary Stillwell, a young woman employed in his factory. He carried his enthusiasm for electricity even into his home and nicknamed his first two children "Dot" and "Dash," from the signals of the telegraph.

In money matters Edison was as reckless as in his expense of time. He employed no bookkeeper, and paid his bills with notes. He rarely knew whether he was in debt or had a surplus on hand. In his view, money was for a means for carrying on the work that was for him the one important thing in life, and he rarely worried about it. He had good reason to have a feeling of security; for it is said that before leaving Newark, he had at one time forty-five distinct inventions in varying stages of completion, and, that the profit arising from their sale amounted to four hundred thousand dollars.

His most important achievement at Newark was the perfecting of the quadruplex telegraph, by means of which not only two but four messages could be sent over one wire at the same instant. Besides this, so many minor inventions were completed that Edison was called "The young man who keeps the path to the patent office hot with his footsteps."

CHAPTER X

"THE WIZARD OF MENLO PARK"

It is probable that when Edison opened his laboratory at Newark he felt that it would be some time before he outgrew that. In 1876, however, his work as an inventor had developed so wonderfully that he decided to give up manufacturing and devote his time wholly to inventing.

He needed a more extensive laboratory, one situated in a place so out of the way of public travel that he would not have many visitors. For the site of his new laboratory, he chose Menlo Park. The name has since come to be so closely associated with Edison that when we hear it mentioned we think of the phonograph, the telephone, the electric light, and all of the great inventions which were worked out there.

It was a quiet spot, about an hour's ride by railroad from New York city, where the inventor was frequently called on business. Here in an open expanse Edison had a modest dwelling and a vast laboratory erected.

This laboratory, a plain white frame structure was far from being a handsome building. Its owner's only wish was to have it spacious, well-lighted and convenient. He spared no cost in fitting it up with the most improved mechanical apparatus for experimenting. He had a powerful engine to supply the force needed.

IN THE LABORATORY

The workshop, a room one hundred feet long, was enough to delight the heart of a lover of fine machinery. There were great whirring, buzzing wheels, endless belts of strongest leather, beautifully finished lathes, milling machines, drills, and planers. There were all sorts of electrical machinery, splendidly made and kept bright and shining. But there were no electric lights and no telephone in the great laboratory unless, perhaps, in the mind of the inventor.

Upstairs was a chemical laboratory, a laboratory far beyond the brightest dreams of the newsboy on the Grand Trunk Railroad. Its walls were lined with shelves laden with rows of mysterious jars and bottles. The inventor made it a rule to keep at hand some of every chemical substance known. There were blowpipes, retorts, test tubes, and flasks without number.

Besides these rooms, there was a library. It was a large one well filled with standard and modern scientific works.

There was a small band of well organized workers at Menlo Park. It included skilled mechanics, with a director at their head; scientific experimenters, with a scholarly professor at their head; a mathematician, a private secretary, and even a bookkeeper.

Guiding and controlling all, was Edison, the wonder worker, who could catch the lightning and hold it imprisoned in tiny glass globes, who could make it possible for one man to hear another talking hundreds of miles away, who could measure the heat of the stars, who could make a machine that would talk and sing and laugh like a human voice.

This man of almost magical powers, who worked at all hours of the night in the lonely laboratory, whence the sound of explosions, and flashes of light more brilliant than sunlight, often issued, began to be regarded almost with a feeling of awe. People called him the "Wizard of Menlo Park."

To those who worked with Mr. Edison, there was nothing awe-inspiring about him. He was not in the least spoiled by his success. He respected all parts of the work to which he had given his devotion, and the man who did the humblest portion of it well, was esteemed by him. He was not afraid of hard work himself, and although he had competent men to manage the business for him, always took an active part in the affairs of the shop. He went about in rusty work clothes stained with acids, and with hands discolored and scarred, inspecting everything, and lending a hand where things were not going just as he wished. Menlo Park was no place for a man who did not love his work so much that he could forget his personal appearance and comfort while busy.

On one occasion a new man refused to perform a task which Mr. Edison had directed him to do. He said that he had not accepted the position with a view of becoming a manual laborer. Mr. Edison with extreme courtesy begged his pardon, for having made an unreasonable request, and then did the work himself. That made the young man feel uncomfortable, but it taught him the lesson which all of Mr. Edison's employees had to learn sooner or later—the lesson of self-forgetfulness in work.

In the management of his business Mr. Edison had conformed in many ways to ordinary business methods. But hours at Menlo Park were almost as irregular as at

Newark. The inventor could not get over the belief that the man who never got so interested in his work that he failed to hear the twelve o'clock whistle at noon, or the six o'clock whistle at night, was a poor sort of fellow. For his own part, he had not outgrown his independence of the clock.

As the years passed, the inventor's mind lost nothing of its youthful activity. He found it easy to keep every one in the big laboratory busy working out his ideas. Whenever he thought of a possible improvement in one of his own inventions, or in a contrivance made by some one else, he made a note of it in a thick blank book. When one piece of work was finished this book always suggested innumerable ideas for further undertakings.

Sometimes Edison's inventions were pushed forward with amazing rapidity. An idea would occur to him in the morning. His draughtsmen would draw up the plans for it, and the workmen would make it in a single day.

He tells an incident to show how quickly he was able to transact patent business, not only at Washington, but in London: He made a discovery at four in the afternoon, telegraphed to his solicitor, and had him draw up the necessary specifications at once. Then he cabled to London, an application for a patent, and before he arose next morning received word that his application had been filed in the English patent office. To understand this speedy transaction, we must remember that while it was early morning at Menlo Park it was noonday at London.

CHAPTER XI

INVENTIONS

While numerous small inventions were thought of, made, and patented in an almost incredibly short space of time, you must not think that Edison never had any hindrances or difficulties. There were inventions on which he and his assistants labored for years, spending tens of thousands of dollars before reaching satisfactory results.

It would take too long to name all of Edison's inventions, and it would be impossible to describe them all. There are very few departments of electrical invention to which he has not contributed something. The electric railroad and the automobile have received a share of his thought. His telephone; the megaphone, which carries the sound of the voice great distances without the help of wires; the quadruplex telegraph; the tasimeter, which measures the heat of the stars; or the kinetoscope,—any one of them would have made the inventor famous. But he is perhaps best known by the invention of the incandescent electric light and the phonograph.

Every American boy and girl has Edison's name

closely associated with the brilliant little globes of light which are seen by thousands, along city streets, in churches, in theaters, in public halls, and even in private dwellings.

A traveler in far off Egypt asked an ignorant donkey boy if he had ever heard of the President of the United States. He had not. He next asked if he had ever heard of Edison. With a nod of intelligence the boy pointed to the electric light before the door of the hotel for answer.

Edison once said that the electric light had cost him more time, anxiety, and expense than any other invention. It was, however, the invention which made him independently rich.

The principle of the light is simple. When an electric current passes from a good conductor to a poor one it causes heat. That a bright light might be obtained by non-conducting substances heated in this way, had been known for many years, but no one before Edison was able to turn the knowledge to practical use.

Even Edison found it extremely difficult to make an inexpensive, durable, and strong light. The greatest difficulty was to find a non-conducting filament strong enough to endure, and slight enough to be heated to a white glow with a moderate charge of electricity.

Those will never forget it, who were present at Menlo Park when the search for the filament was begun. Experiment after experiment failed, while the "wizard," growing only more wide awake and resolute, begged his associates, "Let us make one before we sleep."

Expeditions were made to Japan, India, Africa, and South America in search of the best possible material for the filament.

Men were unwilling to believe that the incandescent electric light could be used extensively for illuminating purposes. But in the winter of 1880, a public exhibit of the new invention was given at Menlo Park. The streets and trees were brilliantly lighted, and the laboratory was aglow inside and out with the dazzling white lights. Special trains were run to Menlo Park. Hundreds of people went to see the novel spectacle and all who saw were convinced that the incandescent light was a success.

The phonograph, while not so familiar to us as the electric light, arouses our wonder even more. You have perhaps heard that sound is made by vibrations of air. You have shouted in a bare room and heard the echo of your words come back with startling distinctness. The wall received the vibrations and sent back other vibrations making similar but somewhat blurred sounds. This repetition of the vibrations to get a repetition of sound is the principle on which the phonograph is based.

Edison gives an interesting account of the dawning of the idea in his mind. He says: "I was singing to the mouthpiece of a telephone, when the vibrations of the voice sent the fine steel point into my finger. That set me to thinking. If I could record the actions of the point and send the point over the same surface afterward, I saw no reason why the thing would not talk. I tried the

Each Phonograph bears my
signature without it no other
machine is genuine

Thomas A Edison

experiment first on a strip of telegraph paper, and found
that the point made an alphabet. I shouted the words
'Halloo! Halloo!' into the mouthpiece, ran the paper
back over the steel point, and heard a faint 'Halloo!
Halloo!' in return. I determined to make a machine
that would work accurately, and gave my assistants
instructions, telling them what I had discovered."

CHAPTER XII

AT ORANGE, NEW JERSEY

In 1886 a new laboratory was built at Orange, New Jersey. This laboratory is so large that it makes its famous predecessor at Menlo Park seem small and insignificant, by comparison. The equipment is complete for carrying on all sorts of experiments from those relating to the kinetograph to those in connection with the magnetic-ore separator.

THE LABORATORY AT ORANGE

In building his laboratory the inventor remembered to provide in many ways for the comfort and pleasure of the men whom he employed. At the top of the building there is a large lecture hall. There the men often assemble to listen to scientific lectures given by the best scholars and lecturers in the country.

A CORNER IN THE LIBRARY

The library, with its wealth of books, is an attractive room. Mr. Edison cares little for luxury or ease, and this room was at first as plain as the rest of the building. But on his forty-second birthday his men surprised him by introducing into his library some of the comforts he never thought of providing for himself. Rugs, easy chairs, tables, pictures, even plants were used to give the room an air of comfort and beauty.

In this room the inventor sometimes sits, not

reading at his ease, but surrounded by great stacks of books on some particular subject, glancing eagerly through one volume after another as if his life depended on his mastering their contents within a given time. He respects books as the record of the labor of other students and scientists. But he is often disappointed in them; he says, "Some way I never find just what I want in books."

During his early manhood, Edison contributed little in person to the social side of life. He believed that in his inventions he gave to the world the best part of himself. Society accepted the inventions but was not satisfied. Men insist on considering a man greater than any machine he may make. Everything Edison did only made people more anxious to see and know him. For a long time he rebuffed all efforts of the public to make a hero of him. When an attempt was made to give a dinner in honor of the great inventor he refused to be present saying: "One hundred thousand dollars would not tempt me to sit through two hours of personal glorification."

Efforts have been made to induce him to talk into one of his phonographs. But he refuses emphatically, declaring, "It would make me sick with disgust to see on every corner, 'Put a nickel in the slot and hear Edison talk.' "

He has not worked in order that he may at one time live without work. He says that his highest pleasure is in work and he looks forward to no season of rest. Although he is so devoted to his work, Edison's life is not void of brightness. He is one of the most joyous men in the world. Failures and disappointments, he has accepted through life as philosophically as he did the destruction of his first laboratory by the angry railroad conductor.

EDISON'S HOME IN LLEWELLYN PARK

He has the rare ability of transferring his attention quickly from one thing to another. When exhausted with work, he will dash out of his office, tell a funny story, have a good laugh with a friend, and in five minutes be as hard at work as ever. He keeps an organ in his library on which he has taught himself to play a few of his favorite airs, and this often affords him a few minutes' refreshment in the midst of hours of close study.

His work never loses its charm; he is always engaged in some novel and interesting experiment. Within the last few years, however, he has admitted some pleasures into his life not directly connected with his work. Mr. Edison has traveled extensively in America and in Europe and been received with high honors everywhere. His first wife having died, he married again, and bought a beautiful and luxurious home in Llewellyn Park, near Orange, New Jersey.

CPSIA information can be obtained
at www.ICGtesting.com
Printed in the USA
FSHW04n1656040418
46290FS